ANDERSONVILLE

ANDERSONVILLE

The Complete Original Screenplay by

David W. Rintels

Introduction by James M. McPherson

Author of *Battle Cry of Freedom*

Foreword by John Frankenheimer

GIDEON
BOOKS

In association with Louisiana State University Press, Baton Rouge

*

Cover photo and photos on pages 18, 23, 32, 41, 61, 84, 133, 134, 139, 166
by Doug Hyun. © 1994 Turner Pictures Inc.

Special vintage-styled Polaroid images on pages 28, 95, 112, 159, 165, 172, 173, 175,
176, 178, by Jim McHugh. © 1994 Turner Pictures Inc.

Book design and production by Mike Burton

To Vicki —

For the Last Best 17 Years of My Life

✳

FOREWORD

John Frankenheimer

Andersonville is the most difficult film I ever directed. David Rintels'
script—thoroughly researched, meticulously written and carefully
structured—was, from page one, a director's proving ground. First,
there are in this film a tremendous number of characters, each of whom
had to be fleshed out, individualized, and made a living person. Second, the very nature of the subject matter itself—a prisoner of war
camp during the Civil War—presents enormous difficulties in realization, staging and dramatic build. Third, the American public for the
most part has never heard of Andersonville—therefore it was necessary not only to dramatize but to explain what the situation was, and
to make believable the horrors that the men went through. At the same
time, it was imperative to preserve the integrity of Rintels' script, which
was telling a true story. That story is a depressing one—thousands of
Union troops were incarcerated in this inhuman place. Many thousands died and many more thousands were transferred to other prison
camps, where they waited out the war. Our story had to find the human drama underneath these events. David wanted to tell a story of
nobility, of courage, and I, as a director, had to find and dramatize
those moments in terms of camera, performance, set design and the
general look of the picture. Finding ways for the many characters to be
interwoven throughout the drama and for the audience to recognize in
a moment who these men were was a formidable task. Staging the
many scenes that David wrote with some kind of variety and energy
was foremost in my mind. We constructed a set which was essentially
a rectangle of nine acres. There were hardly any interiors, so conse-
quently every scene required hundreds, sometimes thousands of extras
in the background and even at times in the foreground. While there

were not many action scenes, those that we have were enormously difficult. The huge riot two-thirds of the way through the film involves over two thousand people. It is, arguably, one of the biggest hand-to-hand fights ever filmed. The escape through the woods had to be exciting, yet not dramatically phony—for our principal actors were indeed caught. I found that I had to work very hard with David to find the rhythm of the film—to orchestrate the highs and lows. David said to me during the production that he didn't want to sacrifice history to drama and I, as a director, had to respect that; nevertheless, drama is my business and I tried to build it wherever I could find it.

David and I worked very closely throughout the filming. I owe him a tremendous amount. I have great admiration for him as a man of integrity and taste and also as a fine writer. This published version of the script represents more or less the final draft. It reflects our endless conferences and discussions and David's revisions over a period of close to a year. I hope the film does it justice.

Australia, Fall 1995   *John Frankenheimer*

ACKNOWLEDGMENTS

Writing for film is only partly the lonely and private process we writers like to claim it is. From the moment an idea is hatched until the final shooting is done on the film itself, a script is read and commented on and praised and criticized by others, and it is revised and made better (or at least different) by the writer. Ideas come from executives, colleagues, actors, grips, anyone who gets his or her hands on it. Often the comments are extremely helpful and illuminating and a writer will be smart to embrace them and make them part of the script, as I have tried to do in *Andersonville*. On occasion the comments are less helpful and then it is up to the writer to ignore them if he can and resist them if he must.

When a script is to be published, the process is different. Here, and only here, the writer has the Last Word. That seems to me to be fair. When a picture is to be made, a writer owes it to his colleagues to give them as much help as he can. If a director wants a scene changed in ways he thinks will make it better or more dramatic or interesting, or if an actor has trouble with a line, or a production manager screams we can't afford to do it this way, a writer should listen carefully and if possible attempt to accommodate them. Ours is a famously collaborative business and no one has a monopoly on wisdom and truth.

But when the script is published just to be read, not filmed, the writer is on his own.

I spent three years on this script and this is the version I like best. It includes a number of scenes and moments which for one reason or another—time, cost, editing, whatever—are not in the final picture.

Along the way, I was involved with some extremely creative and talented people.

There is no more exciting, no more visual, no more in-charge director than John Frankenheimer, director of such classic films as *The Manchurian Candidate, Birdman of Alcatraz* and *Seven Days in May.* John brings words to life with unparalleled energy and passion. (Compare, for example, how I wrote the first scene of the picture, calling for one tempo, with how John directed it. He was absolutely right.) It would be hard to think of another director who could have given as much to this whole enterprise as John did.

Ethel Winant, my associate on numerous projects over the years, has the keenest vision around when it comes to story, and on other things as well. She is incomparable.

The people who work for Ted Turner, whose own personal passion for the Civil War and whose interest in doing a movie about Andersonville got this enterprise off the ground, were extremely helpful throughout. I am particularly indebted to Allen Sabinson, and also benefited from the advice of his associate Howard Cohen and, in an early phase, of Laurie Pozmantier.

From the day I began work I had continuous assistance from the dedicated employees of the National Park Service who administer Andersonville National Historical Site. Park Manager Fred Boyles and Park Ranger Alan Marsh and their associates answered every inquiry and call for help quickly and thoughtfully and with the determination to help me keep this script historically accurate. In particular, Park Ranger Mark Ragan saw me through several early drafts when he was at Andersonville and helped make me aware of many of the thousand details about life there in 1864–5.

In the production of the picture Diane Smith, Nick Lombardo and Jim Wilberger performed with the skill of battlefield commanders which, considering the amazing logistical problems of the picture, I'm sure they felt like at times. We benefited from a fine cast and crew. All of us were in absolute awe of the Civil War Re-Enactors and their dedication to what they do; they were essential to the picture.

Jackie Tone has willingly and painstakingly typed, proofed and cared about this script forever, recently with the able assistance of Magee Marshall. I am very grateful to them as well.

September, 1995   *David W. Rintels*

INTRODUCTION

James M. McPherson

The best of many good things about *Andersonville* is its absolute integrity. There is no glamorization of war here. Quite the contrary; the pain and filth and evil and suffering and dying are depicted with grim realism. The reader can almost smell the stench of this prison camp in which, by August 1864, 33,000 Union POW's were crowded into a space of 25 acres—32 square feet per man—without shade in a deep South summer and with no shelter except what they could rig from blankets, tent flies, and odd bits of cloth. Trigger-happy guards, a rapacious gang of prisoners (the Raiders) who prey on their fellows, primitive sanitation, polluted water, inadequate medical care—all of the things that caused a hundred or more prisoners to die every day during the worst weeks of that terrible summer are vividly portrayed in this gripping drama.

But amid this shocking inhumanity the principal protagonists demonstrate dignity and courage. In an environment that turned some men into beasts and others into zombies, Josiah, McSpadden, Sweet, Gleason, and the others who carry this story retain their essential humanity. They are decent men, good men who defy the evil that surrounds them. Theirs is a story not merely of survival, but of survival with honor.

At the same time this is not a pure morality play that demonizes Confederates and romanticizes Union victims. We meet humane Confederates and evil Yankees. Andersonville was not Auschwitz. The appalling conditions at this POW stockade in a remote corner of southwest Georgia were not the result of deliberate design. Although Henry Wirz, the prison commandant, was the only person tried and executed for war crimes after the American Civil War, the question whether he was really guilty of anything more than inefficiency, bad temper, and petty cruelty remains controversial. Like the 13,000 prisoners who died at Andrsonville and the 32,000 who survived with indelible physical or psychological scars, Wirz was a victim of forces largely beyond his control in this fourth year of a grinding war: shortages of food, medicine, doctors, tools, and supplies of all kinds as Confederates fought a desperate and losing cause in which scarce resources went to their armies rather than to their prisons.

How did things come to such a pass? Early in the Civil War the two sides had negotiated a cartel for the exchange of prisoners captured in battle. Until 1863 this policy worked reasonably well. The few POW camps held men for a relatively brief time until they were exchanged. But in 1863 this process broke down. The main cause of its collapse was the Confederacy's response to the North's enlistment of black soldiers. The Confederate government announced that captured black troops and their white officers would be subject to the death penalty for "inciting slave insurrections." In actual practice no slave insurrections occurred and the Confederacy did not officially execute black captives—though on several occasions Southern troops massacred black Union soldiers who were trying to surrender.

The Confederacy did refuse to exchange captured black soldiers, however, and returned many of them to slavery or put them to hard labor on Confederate fortifications. In protest against this treatment of men who wore the uniform of the United States army, the Union government suspended the cartel until Confederates agreed to exchange black as well as white captives. But the Confederate exchange commissioner vowed that his government would "die in the last ditch" before "giving up the right to send slaves back to slavery as property recaptured."

By the fall of 1863 this impasse had begun to fill up the makeshift POW camps on both sides. In April 1864 Union General-in-Chief Ulysses S. Grant reiterated his government's policy: "No distinction whatever will be made in the exchange between white and colored prisoners . . . Non-acquiescence by Confederate authorities . . . will be regarded as a refusal on their part to agree to the further exchange of prisoners." Confederate authorities did not acquiesce.

The heavy fighting in the spring and summer of 1864 poured an unprecedented number of prisoners into hastily built and inadequate POW camps in both North and South. Because the Confederacy had less of everything than the Union—men, medicine, food, tools, building materials—prison conditions in the South were worse than in the North. Union prisoners in Confederate stockades suffered a death rate

28 percent higher than Confederate prisoners in Union camps. Andersonville was by far the largest Southern prison. More than two-fifths of all Northern prisoners who died during the war died at Andersonville, even though the prison there was not opened until February 1864. Their graves, marked and registered after the war by Clara Barton (founder of the American Red Cross) were a cause of Northern bitterness toward the South for decades after 1865 and serve today as a silent symbol of the barbarism of war.

David Rintels' purpose in this script for a television movie is not to tell the story of POW's in the Civil War or even to chronicle the history of Andersonville. His purpose, in a sense, is higher than that: to dramatize the human epic of Andersonville through the experiences of a dozen or so mostly fictional characters who are based on composites of real persons. Rintels has read the diaries and memoirs of Andersonville prisoners. He has studied the official reports and other evidence. Using his extraordinary skills as a playwright and scriptwriter who has won numerous awards, he brings these dusty documents to life in a riveting script that readers simply will not be able to put down. Here are all the elements of a compelling adventure story that also happens to be true and full of deeper moral meaning: battle and capture; the shock of revelation when first entering the stockade; escape through a tunnel and recapture; clashes with the Raiders and eventual victory over them, with the execution of their six ringleaders after a dramatic trial; rumors of exchange and the poignant awareness that it will never happen; the bonding of good men against evil; the deaths of half of these men and the survival of the rest who keep alive some hope for the redemption of the human race.

This screenplay is not just for Civil War buffs. It is for everyone.

Turner Pictures Presents

A John Frankenheimer / David W. Rintels Film

Written and Produced by
DAVID W. RINTELS

Directed by
JOHN FRANKENHEIMER

Executive Producers
ETHEL WINANT   JOHN FRANKENHEIMER

Co-Producer
DIANE SMITH

Casting by
MARSHA KLEINMAN, C.S.A.

Music by
GARY CHANG

Edited by
PAUL RUBELL, A.C.E.

Production Design by
MICHAEL Z. HANAN

Costume Designer
MAY ROUTH

Director of Photography
RIC WAITE, A.S.C.

ANDERSONVILLE

CAST

Josiah Day	JARROD EMICK
Sergeant McSpadden	FREDERIC FORREST
Martin Blackburn	TED MARCOUX
Trimble	TOM ALDREDGE
Hopkins	CARMEN ARGENZIANO
Billy	JAYCE BARTOK
Collins	FREDERICK COFFIN
Sergeant John Gleason	CLIFF DE YOUNG
Mad Matthew	DENIS FOREST
Tyce	JUSTIN HENRY
Tucker	TONY HIGGINS
2nd Wisconsin	KRIS KAMM
Tobias	ANDREW KAVOVIT
Olek Wisnovsky	OLEK KRUPA
Colonel Chandler	WILLIAM H. MACY
Ethan	MATT MC GRATH
Limber Jim	PETER MURNIK
Bob Reese	GABRIEL OLDS
60th Ohio	TIM PARATI
Munn	WILLIAM SANDERSON
Dick Potter	GREGORY SPORLEDER
Captain Wirz	JAN TRISKA
Thomas Sweet	TOM WILSON

Lieutenant Barrett	BRUCE EVERS
Curtis	MICHAEL HARRINGTON
Patrick Shay	BLAKE HERON
Samson	ROBERT DAVID HALL
Benton	BRUCE WINANT
Captain Sills	JUDSON VAUGHN
Captain Russell	STEPHEN AYERS
Lieutenant Oliver	TIM BLACK
Colonel O'Neil	CLANCY IMISLUND
Georgie	GARY LEE DAVIS
Grundy	SCOTT BRANTLEY
Sarsfield	MICHAEL HAYNES
Sullivan	LONNIE SMITH
Delaney	BUD DAVIS
Willens	CHARLES LAWLOR
Sergeant of the Artillery	KYLE HESTER
Lieutenant Dahlgren	BRETT RICE
Young Guard #1	CHRIS ALLEN
Young Guard #2	MICHAEL BERRY LOWRY
10th Kentucky Corporal	KENNETH PAUL JONES
Guard	JEFF TAFFET
17th Maine Corporal	RICK ROGERS
17th Maine Private	LENNY HERB
Guard with Bayonet	TOM EVEN
Confederate Private	JAMES LEGGAT
Confederate Private	JAMES VAN HARPER
Confederate Corporal	ALEX VAN
Aide	TOM HARPER
Major Sowell	JAMES MAYBERRY
Ethan's Friend #1	JASON ASTORS
Ethan's Friend #2	MICHAEL FLANNERY
Hub	D. HENDERSON BAKER
Patrick Shay's Friend	SEAN CONSIDINE
Old Prisoner #1	BILL GRIBBLE
Old Prisoner #2	STEVE COULTER
Jury Foreman	ANDREW STAHL

The Sergeants

BRUCE STEPHEN RYON
GARY B. CARPENTER
KENN DRESCHER
SAMUEL L. "BIG STEVE" STEPHENS
JASON W. MAY
C. ALAN RAWLINS, SR.
JOE TROTTER
THOMAS E. WILLIAMS
JAMES BURKHART
TROY ANDREW COOL
MARK S. FAULKNER
MARTIN "BANJO MAN" LIEBSCHNER, JR.
MATTHEW MURDZAK
TIM KUEBERTH
ROBERT E. WESTMAN

ANDERSONVILLE

Fade In:

Ext.   The Gentle Wooded Hills of Virginia — Day

PANNING SLOWLY FROM A HILLTOP across the magnificent countryside. Hills, trees, open valleys. Now, to disturb the summer peace, the heavy SOUND of distant artillery, and then CLOSER SCATTERED cannon and musket fire. Birds fly up. A deer bounds away.

TITLE CARD: COLD HARBOR, VIRGINIA

Ext.   In the Woods — Day

A minor skirmish in the woods. A small and irregular line of Union foot soldiers (Company I, 19th Massachusetts Volunteers) is kneeling or standing behind trees, exchanging sporadic fire with a few Confederates—unseen except for a glimpse of grey and an occasional musket flash—in the thickets.

TITLE CARD: JUNE 1, 1864

Walking calmly behind his men, SGT. McSPADDEN, a First Sergeant, an old-timer, keeps an eye on things. The Civil War is starting its fourth year and McSpadden is not going to get excited at the likes of this. He stops and looks up at—

A Signal Tower on a Nearby Hill

A large elevated platform, a quickly-built but substantial log-and-earthworks structure. Union men on its top lower one flag, raise another.

Sgt. McSpadden

—sees the flags and then checks his own area. Satisfied, he goes quickly to—

—JOSIAH DAY, a good soldier, a printer by trade, at 23 a corporal and veteran of the entire war.

> McSPADDEN
> Josie, lad—go tell the Captain—there's only a few of
> 'em—we can swing around and drive 'em—
> *(makes a long left-to-right loop)*
> —right into his arms—in five minutes unless he tells
> us no.

Right, Sergeant. Josiah is quickly off, left to right, passing a couple of others in his company—TUCKER, a young Boston tailor, THOMAS SWEET, a huge and gentle baby-faced farm boy, and BOB REESE, Josiah's cousin and best friend—as he lopes at a measured pace through the woods.

CAMERA MOVES WITH HIM and shows a young man doing his job with neither fear nor bravado.

The musket fire is not close, not dangerous—still, he does stop briefly to make sure before crossing a clearing—and then he continues to—

A Stone Wall

—where another veteran Company of the same Regiment is waiting behind the wall, not in combat. Their uniforms, like Josiah's, are long on use, short on niceties. Hearing something coming through the woods, they quickly bring their muskets up on—

—Josiah emerging from the woods. The men relax as Josiah goes to CAPTAIN RUSSELL, 50-years-old, a bearded officer who is with LT. OLIVER. With plenty of breath left . . .

> JOSIAH
> Sergeant says there's just a few of 'em, sir—we can
> swing around and drive 'em into you—five minutes
> 'less you tell him not to.

DURING THIS, A SHARP RATTLE OF MUSKETRY from where Josiah has come. It gives the Captain pause.

> CAPTAIN RUSSELL
> I don't know there's any such a few of them.
> *(then—)*
> See any on your way over?

> JOSIAH
> No sir.

> CAPTAIN RUSSELL
> See any cavalry?

> JOSIAH
> No sir.

> LT. OLIVER
> You know ol' Jim McSpadden, sir. He says he'll drive
> 'em, he'll drive 'em.

MORE SHOOTING causes the Captain to hesitate again—until the Lieutenant's look says pretty good wall we're behind here. So—

> CAPTAIN RUSSELL
> All right. Tell him to drive away.

> JOSIAH
> Yes sir.

And Josiah is off, back where he came from, as we HOLD the Captain and Lieutenant. . . .

> CAPTAIN RUSSELL
> Long as there's no cavalry.

The Lieutenant nods, moves quickly among the men.

> LT. OLIVER
> Get ready boys, they're coming in from over there.

Ext. Resume Josiah Running in the Woods — Day

Right to left, passing the same identifiable trees as on the way over. The MUSKET FIRE is still not close and Josiah is running easi—

BANG! THUNK! A bullet knocks off his cap, spins him down and around, smashes into a tree he's passing. Josiah bounces down on the ground, his face bleeding, grabs for the musket he's dropped, is about to pick it up when he SEES—

—One, two . . . six . . . Confederate infantry, hard types, run in, muskets ready. Confederate Cavalryman MAJOR SOWELL, on horseback as are two others, rides up, holding a pistol on Josiah.

> MAJOR SOWELL
> Leave it there.

Josiah hesitates. He looks around for a place to run, SEES—

—two more Southern Cavalrymen wheel in hard on their horses, carbines ready, covering his possible escape route.

There's no choice. Josiah lays his musket back on the ground, straightens up.

> MAJOR SOWELL
> Put him over with the others.

Sowell and the other horsemen race off. Two of the Rebel infantry march Josiah away.

Ext.   In the Woods (The Original Location) — Day

—where McSpadden, wounded in the shoulder, is sitting on the ground, being bandaged by Bob Reese. Around them, seven or eight Union soldiers—Tucker, Sweet, several from other Companies—sit on the ground, weaponless, under Confederate Infantry Guard.

WE SEE two more Massachusetts Prisoners: BILLY, 19, an innocent, and the usually tense, usually angry TYCE, a loner who stays a fair distance away from the others.

[4]

In the clearing, a few yards away, are several Union dead.

Josiah is marched in under guard and told to sit near the wounded McSpadden and Bob Reese.

> BOB REESE
> Cousin? Are you hurt?

> JOSIAH
> No. Are you?
> *(no)*
> How are you, Sergeant?

> MCSPADDEN
> Scratch.

From his position behind McSpadden, bandaging McSpadden's shoulder, Bob Reese looks privately at Josiah—No, it's no scratch.

> MCSPADDEN
> Not such a few as I thought, eh, lads?
> *(shaking his head)*
> Sorry excuse for a Sergeant I am, not even knowing there was horses in the neighborhood . . . Deaf and blind, deaf and blind.

Josiah looks at one of their dead at the edge of the woods.

> JOSIAH
> Is that James?

> BOB REESE
> *(and over there . . .)*
> And Benjamin.

Hard news, borne stoically. Their fellow prisoners—Sweet, the huge farm boy, and Tucker, the anxious tailor—are depressed and sorrowing or, like Tyce, sullen, on edge.

Billy manages a small, sorrowful, friendly gesture for Josiah. We've had better days than this one, hey Josie . . . ?

Captain Russell and the wounded Lt. Oliver, now also prisoners, are marched into camp by a rude infantryman and ordered to sit.

Major Sowell rides into camp at the head of his small troop of Southern Cavalry. He surveys the scene, then confers privately with a hard-eyed CONFEDERATE CORPORAL, a foot soldier. Now he trots over to Captain Russell and salutes.

> MAJOR SOWELL
> My respects, Captain. If you'll detail two of your men, I know you'll want to bury your dead.

> CAPTAIN RUSSELL
> We do, sir. I thank you.

Russell looks over to his men. Josiah and Bob Reese get up unbidden—we'll do it—and go with two Confederate infantry.

> MAJOR SOWELL
> You'll be staying here tonight and moving on in the morning. You have rations and blankets for your men?

Captain Russell looks to McSpadden, who tells him—

> MCSPADDEN
> Our haversacks are over there, sir.

> MAJOR SOWELL
> *(to the Corporal)*
> Have them brought over.

> CONFEDERATE CORPORAL
> Yes sir.

Major Sowell salutes Captain Russell and leads his horsemen away fast, leaving the Prisoners in the guard of the Infantry, and especially the cold-eyed Corporal, who tells the Prisoners . . .

CONFEDERATE CORPORAL

You all lie flat on the ground. Nobody stands, nobody
moves around 'til morning.

He posts Guards around the perimeter, four or five of them . . .

. . . as Josiah and Bob Reese dig graves for their friends under guard a
few yards away. . . .

Ext.   Full Shot of the Group — Day

A small, silent group as they lie flat on the ground. There is nothing
heroic about this, about any of it.

Same Scene — Night

Watchful Southern guards, all infantrymen.

Billy, lying on his stomach, is feeding little twigs into a small campfire.

The Other Union Prisoners are lying on the ground near the fire, cov-
ered by blankets against the cold, mostly sleeping, a couple talking
quietly among themselves. Josiah lies next to Bob Reese, near the
sleeping McSpadden.

CLOSE on Josiah and Bob Reese, all in a whisper . . .

JOSIAH

Cousin?
                    (what?)
Did you ever think?

BOB REESE

I never did. Did you?

JOSIAH

No, never.

BOB REESE

I never would've given, but there was too many of
'em.
                - (MORE) -

[7]

BOB REESE (cont.)
(I know . . .)
What do we do?

JOSIAH
Pick our time and make a run for it.

BOB REESE
Now?

JOSIAH
They're all watching.

BOB REESE
(But) it's night.
(then—)
Once they get you in their prison camps, they got
you good.
(I know . . .)
Here's what . . . Going to stand up slow . . . say I have
to relieve myself . . . they'll send a guard with me . . .
knife in my pocket . . . when they hear and come after
me, you run for it. Run like the devil . . . the farm
with the smokehouse we passed this morning . . . ?
looks like Uncle John's . . . ?
(yes)
Meet you there. . . .

JOSIAH
Who'll look after the Sergeant . . . ?

McSPADDEN
Give my love to all the pretty ladies in Boston. . . .

Because his eyes are closed, we thought he was asleep.

JOSIAH
We will, Sergeant. . . .

BOB REESE
Ready?

Josiah nods. A moment and then Bob Reese starts to stand easily, obviously, unthreateningly, calling out as he does . . .

> BOB REESE
> Got to relie . . .

BANG! Before he is up, Bob Reese is dead, shot through the head. His body falls across Billy, onto his head, on his face. Billy shouts in horror and rolls back into the campfire and then has to slap embers off his head and arms—

—while in the same moment Josiah starts to jump up. McSpadden grabs his arm and holds him in a steel grip.

> McSPADDEN
> No, lad! Sit. Sit.

> CONFEDERATE CORPORAL
> *(easily, simply)*
> Told you. Nobody stands, nobody moves around.

All the other guards are at the ready with leveled muskets as the Corporal reloads.

The horror to Josiah and McSpadden, to Captain Russell, especially to Billy, is the greater for its calmness.

Ext.   Country Road — Late Afternoon

A long, empty, dusty dirt highway . . . and now, from around a bend, comes the column of prisoners under guard. IN LONG SHOT WE SEE there are a few more than before, maybe 50 now, from Massachusetts I Company and from other Units, all guarded by six familiar Southern Infantrymen . . .

. . . and AS WE SEE THEM TRUDGE INTO CAMERA Josiah, still ashen-faced from the night's events, supporting the limping, laboring McSpadden . . . Tucker and Sweet, the huge farm boy, carrying someone on his back . . . Billy, head down and shaking, stumbling along far behind Josiah . . . Captain Russell walking next to the wounded Lt. Oliver . . . the others from the camp. They have been marched a long way and are dusty, tired, thirsty. Most of them have slung sacks—haversacks—over a shoulder.

As they come, CLOSER SHOT on Josiah and McSpadden and, directly in front of them, Captain Russell. Josiah gives McSpadden and Sweet water from his canteen—they are careful to take only one swallow each—and then Josiah, uncertain of the etiquette, offers it to Captain Russell, who hesitates before gratefully taking it.

> CAPTAIN RUSSELL
> Thank you, Day . . . I lost mine (back there someplace). . . .

> LT. OLIVER
> Very kind of you, Day.

> CAPTAIN RUSSELL
> Your cousin had a wife back in New Bedford. . . .

> JOSIAH
> Yes, sir. And little boy.

> CAPTAIN RUSSELL
> You give me their address so I can write them.

> JOSIAH
> Yes, sir. I know they'll appreciate it. . . .

Josiah comes back to McSpadden who tells him privately—

> MCSPADDEN
> Better keep an eye on Billy. . . .

Josiah looks over his shoulder at Billy stumbling blindly along by himself and shaking his head from side to side. . . .

In High Full Shot the Camera Hinges Them All to an Intersection Where, Waiting for Them, Surprisingly —

—WE SEE sitting on the ground another and bigger group of Yankee prisoners under guard, 200 or more, dustier, more tired, more heavily watched, waiting at a country railroad track. Our group moves in and sits or collapses between 2nd WISCONSIN, a bespectacled young storekeeper, and 60th OHIO, a bearded older frontiersman.

2ND WISCONSIN

19th Massachusetts? . . . 2nd Wisconsin. You were on our left second day at Gettysburg.

TUCKER

I remember. They couldn't move you.

2ND WISCONSIN

Tried hard enough though, didn't they . . . ?
(indicates some nearby prisoners)
They were on Cemetery Ridge. Gave that place its rightful name.

60TH OHIO

When'd they get you boys?

SWEET

Yesterday . . . back there.

2ND WISCONSIN

Know where they're taking us? Won't tell us a thing.

As the new prisoners sit among the old, some are silent, some sullen, a couple exchange small talk—You wouldn't have any water in that canteen, would you, friend? . . . Where'd they catch you at? Who you with? . . .

. . . as Josiah makes sure McSpadden is comfortable on the ground. McSpadden's shoulder causes him to wince in spite of himself. Now Josiah looks over to where—

—Billy sits alone, removed and remote, head down, shaking.

Josiah

Looks to McSpadden, who nods approval for Josiah to deal with this. Josiah walks over to Billy, hunkers down next to him.

> JOSIAH
> How you farin', Billy?

Billy shakes his head from side to side.

> BILLY
> Last night. Last night . . . last night . . . last night . . . .

Josiah is silent. But he looks up when he HEARS—

Josiah's Pov of Confederate Captain Sills

CAPTAIN SILLS is in overall charge. He speaks to the Prisoners—

> CAPTAIN SILLS
> You new men—I know some of you haven't eaten today—we're sorry but we don't have anything here, for you or for us either—we've sent to town for a wagonfull—just please be patient, all right?

The Prisoners

A couple of the sullen ones grumble—Tyce, noticeably—but most of the men accept it. Fair enough.

> 60TH OHIO
> Sure hope they're quick about it—ain't et since yesterday—my bellybutton's rubbin' up against my backbone.

Resume Josiah, Billy

Josiah looks back to Billy.

> JOSIAH
> You come over here, Billy—stay with me and the Ser-
> geant. I'm going to need you to help me with him.

He starts off. Dumbly, automatically, Billy gets up and follows Josiah
back to McSpadden, silently sits next to them.

Now Josiah takes some paper and a crude pencil out of his haversack
and settles down among his friends.

HOLD Josiah CLOSE as he struggles to think of words to write. He
can't come up with them. Then—

Resume Group

> 2ND WISCONSIN
> Here she comes.

The men look eagerly to the road where—

Their POV of a Coach and Team

A black Coachman in full livery is driving a handsome open carriage
with FOUR attractive YOUNG LADIES in nice day dresses down the
dusty road toward the Prisoners.

Intercut the Prisoners

Watching them approach, unhappy it's not the food wagon. Josiah
looks up from his unstarted letter as Tyce grumbles—

TYCE
Nothin' for us.

Full Shot of the Carriage and the Officers

As the carriage arrives and stops, the gallant Captain Sills sweeps off
his hat and bows low.

                     CAPTAIN SILLS
Good afternoon, ladies.

                     YOUNG LADIES
Good afternoon to you, Captain.

                     CAPTAIN SILLS
Fine day for a ride in the country.
               (certainly is, Captain)
We have some uninvited visitors we're just escorting
out of your neighborhood.

                     YOUNG LADY #1
Very thoughtful of you, Captain.

                CONFEDERATE PRIVATE #1
Hey, Captain! Maybe the ladies'd like to inspect the
Prisoners. Prob'ly never seen a Yank close up.

The Prisoners are anything but happy at this suggestion, at being on
exhibition.

The Young Ladies consider the idea, confer among themselves,
giggle—and reluctantly decline.

                 CONFEDERATE CORPORAL
Hey—Yank—get on your feet. You're in the presence
of fine Southern ladies here.

The Prisoners don't budge. They are growing unhappier.

> CONFEDERATE CORPORAL
> Maybe the ladies'd like to hear 'em sing a song,
> Captain. . . .

When the Young Ladies seem intrigued by that possibility, Captain Sills turns to the Prisoners.

> CAPTAIN SILLS
> Will you favor the ladies with a song, gentlemen?

> CONFEDERATE PRIVATE #1
> Make 'em sing Dixie, Cap'n!

The Prisoners are getting angrier.

The Guards are relaxed, egging them on easily.

> CONFEDERATE CORPORAL
> You boys can't carry rifles no more. Maybe one of you
> can carry a tune.

New Angle Behind the Prisoners

A CIVILIAN GUARD, an angry farmer standing on the far side of the prisoners, comes up behind the Prisoners and starts to kick them in the back as they sit. He does it quietly so the Captain doesn't hear, just as he doesn't see—

> CIVILIAN GUARD
> Git up. Sing Dixie for the ladies . . . You'uns come
> down here, think you can shoot us'ns, burn us out . . .
> Git up, damn you.

Nobody moves. He goes down the line. Kick. Kick. Vicious kick.

The Ladies, Captain Sills in the Twilight

They don't see or hear what's going on. Neither do the other guards.

In the Ranks

The situation is becoming dangerously tense. Some of the prisoners—including Tyce and 60th Ohio—are becoming enraged. Josiah and McSpadden, sitting next to each other, exchange a what's-going-to-happen-next look.

> TYCE
> *(not loudly)*
> Kicks me, I'll kill him.

McSpadden, two rows in front of the kicker and in no danger himself, struggles to his feet. To the ladies—

> McSPADDEN
> Dixie, you say? I don't believe we know any such song
> as that. Ah, but 'Kathleen Mavoureen'. . .

He starts to sing the most beautiful and deeply moving song of the Civil War, the 'Lili Marlene' of its time, heartbreaking, apolitical, personal.

The situation changes.

The Ladies are touched. No more giggling.

The Captain and uniformed guards, too.

When the song is over the Young Ladies quietly thank the Captain, who silently bows them off. They tell the Coachman to drive on.

The Prisoners watch them go.

Ext.   Same Scene — Night

The Prisoners are eating hungrily by torchlight.

All but Tucker, who is expertly sewing a rent in a shirt, using his shears and a needle-and-thread . . .

. . . and Josiah, who is still sitting with pencil and paper, still trying to think of words that won't come.

McSpadden has been lying down. Now he sits up, tries to move his painful shoulder. To Josiah—

                    McSpadden
Bob's wife?
                    (yes)
I always see you readin' and writin'. . . .

                    Josiah
Letters home. So they don't worry.

                    McSpadden
When you finish that, could I have the loan of your pencil?
                    ('course . . .)
What's it like, being so educated?

                    Josiah
I'm just an apprentice. . . .
                    (then—)
You just realize how much it is you don't know.

                    McSpadden
You go ahead and write. I don't want to bother you.

                    Josiah
My father's a printer. He taught me. And my mother always read to me while I was growing up.

                    McSpadden
Mine'll have to go to the priest to read what I send her. She's never got a letter in her life . . .

You go ahead.

Corporal Josiah Day (played by Jarrod Emick), a member of Company I, 19th Massachusetts Volunteers.

It's another long moment before Josiah begins, with difficulty . . .

JOSIAH'S VOICE OVER

Dear Sarah.

This is the letter I wanted never to write.

Bob was killed last night.

He died in my arms with all our friends around and did not suffer even for a moment.

No man was ever braver or a better companion. Everyone in our Regiment says so.

His love for you and Matthew was . . .

Josiah hears the SOUND OF AN APPROACHING TRAIN, looks up and SEES—

Ext.   The Small Train — Night

Approaching.

Ext.   Full Scene — Night

The Guards start to get the Prisoners up to meet the train. Josiah keeps writing.

Ext.   The Train — Night

Our first clear look. It is a cattle train, a small locomotive with only three cars behind it—two slat-sided, see-through cars followed by a caboose.

Ext.   Full Scene Including Train and Josiah — Night

Josiah continues to write as the men around him quickly gobble the last of the food.

JOSIAH'S VOICE OVER
We are being taken South, where to only the Lord
knows. Please tell my father and mother I am content
- (MORE) -

to leave it in His hands. I will write them whenever I
get where we are going.

He hastily writes an address on an envelope and tells Billy to help him
get the shaky McSpadden to his feet. As the prisoners form up, the
Confederate Captain calls . . .

CAPTAIN SILLS
Enlisted men only . . . Officers over here, please. This
train's not for you.

Concern among the men, and the officers too, at being separated. Josiah and McSpadden share uncertain looks. . . .

Captain Russell

Captain Russell stands on tiptoe, looking anxiously for Josiah and
McSpadden through the standing, milling men.

CAPTAIN RUSSELL
Sergeant! McSpadden! Corporal! Day!

Josiah, McSpadden

They see him and leave Billy to make their way to him through the
moving soldiers. When they get to the Captain he seems . . . a little
awkward, a little moved. Uh . . .

CAPTAIN RUSSELL
How are you Sergeant? How's the should . . . ?

McSPADDEN
Never better, sir.

CAPTAIN RUSSELL
I just want to say—you've both always been good soldiers—always did what had to be done—
(to Josiah)
- (MORE) -

CAPTAIN RUSSELL (cont.)
You don't say much, Day, but I never heard you complain and you always did the hard jobs—

JOSIAH
No more than anyone else, sir.

MCSPADDEN
Pleasure was ours, Captain.

They nod and thank him . . . but the moment is still emotional and a little awkward. In the Silence . . .

JOSIAH
Captain . . . Bob's wife's address is on this. You may have an easier time getting it sent than I would. . . .

CAPTAIN RUSSELL
(takes it)
Where you're going—you take care of the boys now—

MCSPADDEN
Don't worry none, Captain. After three years, the boys can take care of themselves just fine—

CAPTAIN RUSSELL
I just hate like the Devil having to leave 'em . . . We've been through a lot together, haven't we?
(they know)
Well, you're in charge now. Do what you can for 'em.
(to Josiah)
Something happens to the Sergeant, you'll be in command.

JOSIAH
I'll do my best, sir.

CAPTAIN RUSSELL
I know you will.
(calling to the others—)
- (MORE) -

CAPTAIN RUSSELL (cont.)
God bless you, boys!
(then —)
Go along with 'em now.
(to Josiah)
I'll mail your letter.

JOSIAH
Thank you, sir.

McSPADDEN
See you back in Boston on a sun-shiny day, Captain.

Ext.   Men Crowding to Train — Night

The other men moving to the train interpose and separate them when there might still be something left unsaid. The Captain gives a little wave and turns away so Josiah and McSpadden can't see his face.

Fuller Shot

As Josiah and McSpadden and the other enlisted men are herded by the Confederate Guards to the train and Billy comes to rejoin them—

TYCE
Hey, Johnny Reb—tell us where you're taking us.

CONFEDERATE PRIVATE #1
You'll find out soon enough.

The men are herded into the cattle cars, first the first one, then the second, until each car is jammed absolutely solid with prisoners. Josiah needs Billy's help to get McSpadden carefully up and in.

In the cars there's no room to sit, to turn around, no room at all.

DURING THIS WE HEAR THEIR PROTESTS: Watch my arm, y'fool . . . no more, no more, no more . . . Tyce: No more room in here . . . we can't breathe. . . .

June 1864, as prisoners are herded onto the train in Virginia for the journey to Andersonville.

The Guards ignore the protests and force them, jam them, onto the train and slam the doors shut.

The Northern Officers watch, moved, in pain, in silent protest.

Guards get on the roof of the caboose and on the locomotive.

On a signal, the train pulls out, heading South.

The Northern Officers, favoring Captain Russell and Lt. Oliver under guard at the station, watch the train go. They look until—

—the train is out of sight.

Captain Russell sags and shakes his head, deeply moved. He has a premonition and we sense it. . . .

Ext.   Long Shot of the Moving Train — Night

Moving slowly South through the Virginia countryside. *MUSIC IN QUIETLY:* A slow sad banjo playing "THE BATTLE HYMN OF THE REPUBLIC. . . ."

Ext.   Montage The Train — Night/Day

As the train moves slowly, laboriously, South. In a SERIES OF SHOTS Night becomes Day, and then Night again . . .

. . . and *THE MUSIC CONTINUES, NOW SYMPHONICALLY . . .*

. . . as the train passes black field hands who look up from their cotton to watch . . .

. . . through woods and fields . . .

. . . and through a pretty town which does not yet show the ravages of war, and where children stop their play to stare at them. . . .

Int./Ext.   In and On the Train — Night

The men, all standing, jammed together with no room to move or sit, are moaning in thirst and misery . . .

. . . not the stoic Josiah, who looks anxiously to McSpadden, who is not feeling at all well but manages a grin and a shrug for him . . .

. . . as Tyce calls for water, give us some water, you damn Rebs! . . . but there is no water . . .

. . . and some men twist and turn and try to get near the slats to breathe good air . . .

... and Josiah and Billy keep men from leaning against McSpadden's wounded shoulder ...

... and some boost others up to look out ...

... as a parched man tries to find one more drop in a dry canteen and turns to his friend, but his friend's canteen is bone-dry, too ...

... while the Guards look down from the roof of the caboose, at ease behind their guns ...

... and the train's fireman throws on more wood ...

... and Tucker and Sweet twist and turn to peer out the slats, trying to see where they are heading and ...

... it becomes DAY again, and ...

Ext.   The Train — Day

It clacks through woods and then slows and ...

Ext.   The Railroad Station at Andersonville — Day

... the train pulls in and stops on the edge of town. There are Guards here too, waiting to meet the train ...

... and the guards on the train hop down, get ready, and then open the doors. *MUSIC OUT.*

The men fall and stagger out of the train in a state of near collapse. Josiah tells Billy to help him with the now-fevered McSpadden, but they are only three of a large and dirty mob.

As they spill out onto the platform, McSpadden holds up his good arm and calls for—

[25]

—and Tucker and Sweet and Tyce fight to make their way to him and Josiah and Billy, but this attempt at military order is swept aside as their guards take charge and get them into some sort of line.

The guards bracket them and march them two hundred yards down a dusty road through the town of Andersonville—

—although to call Andersonville a "town" is to exaggerate. There are, beside the railroad station, only a half-dozen shabby houses surrounded by woods . . . the whole community nothing more than "a hole cut in the wilderness." The men are marched a short distance (a few hundred yards) to a Stockade Gate and told to Halt.

Close Shots on Josiah, Others

Josiah, supporting McSpadden. He looks up at—all the Prisoners look up at—an enormous and intimidating structure:

Ext.   Prisoners' POV of The Prison — Day

"A massive palisade of great squared logs standing upright in the ground . . . Two massive wooden gates, with heavy iron hinges and bolts."

A 'Star Fort' and Redoubt, the Star Fort with seven cannon, the Redoubt with three, are posted within earthworks, with all the cannon at angles facing the Stockade gates, to cover the whole interior of the prison. They are manned by a troop of watchful artillery.

There are also outside the gates Stocks, medieval devices of imprisonment, at the moment unfilled.

Atop the palisade, elevated sentry boxes—"Turkey Roosts"—each occupied by two Very Young or Very Old Guards (more about them later)—ring the Stockade. The sentry towers are 88 feet apart and accessible only by ladders outside the walls.

The Prisoners at the Stockade Gate

The prisoners are in bad condition and some are visibly anxious as they wait. They look at the cannon and stocks and towers—

—and they look at the closed gates, and they can only imagine what lies beyond.

> 60TH OHIO
>
> Hey, Johnny Reb—where are we?

> GUARD
>
> Georgia.

Two Old Prisoners

—Old not in years but in length of time at Andersonville, young men in tattered Union uniforms, their faces prematurely aging and haggard. They are being herded out of the nearby woods at a fast pace by angry, bayonet-jabbing Confederate Guards and snapping, jumping bloodhounds on leashes—

—and the furious Camp Commandant, HENRY WIRZ, on horseback.

The two Old Prisoners, would-be escapees, are run to the Stocks and clamped in hard and unceremoniously.

> WIRZ
>
> Teach you to run!

The dogs snap at the immobile men even after the Stocks are shut on them.

Captain Henry Wirz (played by Jan Triska), Commandant of Andersonville. Wirz's right arm was in constant pain from the wound he received at the Battle of Seven Pines in Virginia, May 31–June 1, 1862.

Our Men

Looking on, and then looking anxiously at each other.

Dogs. Stocks. Bayonets.

What have we gotten into?

Captain Wirz

Sees the two men clamped into the stocks and then angrily wheels his horse toward the new men at the gate. Wirz is not a big man, not imposing in any way, a man with a small sharp-pointed moustache and full beard, with a wounded right arm which is sometimes bandaged and always a source of pain and misery. He looks down from his horse at the new arrivals and gives the order in a German accent . . .

> WIRZ
>
> Open the gate . . . !

Med. Shot on McSpadden, Josiah, Others (Including Guards)

Josiah is supporting McSpadden and Billy is with them as they move toward the entrance, past the fearsome dogs and the angry Wirz.

As they come, to another GUARD—

> McSPADDEN
> *(croaks)*
> And what do you call this little piece of heaven?

> GUARD
> This? This here's Andersonville.

Full Shot The Prisoners

As the Stockade gate is swung open and the Order to "Forward, March" is given, all the men, FEATURING Josiah supporting McSpadden, Billy and Tucker and Sweet, Tyce and 60th Ohio and 2nd Wisconsin, start into the camp. As they go through the gates, past the dogs and the Guards, past the cannons and the stocks and the towers and the watchful eye of Wirz . . .

Fade Out.

Fade In:

Ext.   Inside Andersonville (Continuing Action) — Day

As Josiah and the others come through the Main Gate (CONTINU-
ING) they stop when they see the following astonishing sights:

Their POV of . . .

Twenty-six thousand (later 33,000) Prisoners, all in Union blue, some
half-naked, some missing arms and legs, a number bearded and long-
haired, many with open sores on their faces and bodies, a number
chained together in one enormous ball-and-chain. About 200, no
more, are Black. For the most part the men are sitting or standing
around their 'shebangs' (jury-rigged tents and a very few, very rough
wooden huts) and doing . . .

. . . little or nothing except talking among themselves as they are without means of recreation or distraction. The only exceptions are a few
men playing with tattered cards and two others playing chess with
pieces carved out of roots and . . .

An Official Sutler . . .

. . . his shed just inside the North Gate, selling food at astronomical
prices, and an occasional Tailor or Barber, plus a Gambler shilling for
a chuck-a-luck game, and various other small for-profit enterprises
such as a laundry . . .

. . . and a Couple of Groups of Men

. . . who are at work digging wells, and some others who are bathing . . .

In the Swamp . . .

. . . a stream sluggish almost to the point of motionlessness which
oozes through the middle of the treeless, sandy, grassless camp and is

the camp's principal source of water as well as the repository of every kind of waste and filth.

The Swamp is at the low centerpoint of the camp, with gently sloping hills going up to the Stockade walls.

The Notorious 'Deadline'

A low post-and-rail fence (posts about 20 feet apart, 19 feet inside the Stockade walls) running along the entire inside perimeter, which no prisoner is allowed to cross on peril of being instantly shot to death.

There are some Negroes, slaves, repairing the Deadline under the eye of a huge and imposing Confederate Sergeant, who is armed with a shotgun and carrying a whip as well.

Many of the Prisoners

. . . on the hillsides look up to SEE who the new men are and some, maybe a hundred, get up to approach the Main Gate for a better look at . . .

Josiah and His Comrades

They are looking at this scene by Breughel out of Dante by Matthew Brady and, more than just looking at it—

—smelling it, for the stench is fearful—

—as they see the hundred approaching Prisoners—

—But first they have to pass by . . .

. . . where the Old Prisoners are waiting for them. The Old men, all with dirty, sooty faces, crowd around the New, anxious for answers and handouts. . . .

The crowded camp, with the Deadline in the foreground. When the camp had almost 33,000 prisoners each had approximately 68 inches by 68 inches of room. Tents were not supplied to the prisoners and were fashioned from materials the men had with them when taken captive. Smoke rises from the cooking fires of men lucky enough to have wood, which was almost impossible to obtain late in the war.

OLD PRISONERS
You boys got any food with you? . . . You was with
Grant in Virginia? How we doin' up there? . . . Anybody from New Jersey? . . . You boys hear anything
about getting exchanged? . . . Got anything you want
to trade? . . . What'll you take for that coat?
(a whisper . . .)
I got eight dollars in greenbacks. . . .

Josiah and the new arrivals, including Tyce and 60th Ohio and 2nd Wisconsin, who may not have felt or looked so good when they came through the gate but are Recruiting Posters compared to these men crowding around them, listen and look at them in bewilderment, especially when . . .

Hey! Don't push!

You were standing on my damn foot!

. . . and Old Prisoner #2 smashes Old Prisoner #1 to the ground with a single punch, business as usual to which the other Old Prisoners don't especially react.

Med. Close of an Old Prisoner

DICK POTTER is on the hill, squinting down at Josiah and the others, hard. Does he recognize them? He lifts a hand which holds one of his crutches and shields his eyes from the sun's glare, trying to focus as . . .

Resume Josiah, McSpadden, Others From Dick's POV

Standing, looking around at the astonishing sights when . . .

Angle on a New Arrival

. . . a confident, cheerful little ferret of a man, MUNN, pushes his way quickly through the crowd to Josiah and the others.

The Old Prisoners fall silent as he gets to Josiah and McSpadden and starts his patter.

>   MUNN
> Hey! Fresh fish! Welcome to Andersonville—
>   *(a generous wave)*
> —fine looking place, don'tcha think? . . . For a hog
> pen, maybe . . . Where'd you get catched at? Virginia
> from the looks of things. . . .
>   *(i.e., the unit designations on their forage caps)*
> That's good. Means Grant's going forward, Bobby
> Lee's going back, just the way we like it . . . Let me

show you around, get you a good place to stay. You
want to be up near the wall, away from the Swamp—
don't stink so bad and there ain't so many bugs—
people neither—

DURING THIS, Munn has been starting to steer . . . not Josiah and
not McSpadden who don't understand what's going on and want to
know more . . . but Tucker and Sweet and Billy, and 60th Ohio and
2nd Wisconsin, who are now permanently affixed as friends to Josiah's
group, when . . .

. . . a crutch JABS Munn hard, very hard, in the chest, knocking him
backwards, and . . .

> DICK
> You get away! I know what you're about, Munn. You
> just get away from them!

Dick Potter, thin as a rail, limping and shirtless, fierce bright eyes and
wild hair and beard, an Old Testament Prophet using his crutch as a
weapon, has come down the hill and taken on Munn—

—to the surprise of Josiah and his friends and the secret, largely un-
spoken approval of the other Old Prisoners around them—

—as the delight of a young man who's lost his mind, MAD MAT-
THEW, who dances around and laughs, happily and inappropriately,
whenever there's trouble—

—as Munn now turns on Dick, deciding whether to fight, but he first
looks for help to where his own allies are—

Featuring the Raiders

—a large group of better-fed, better-dressed Old Prisoners, known as
The Raiders and including two of their six leaders, COLLINS and
CURTIS, too far away to help right now—

—as in CLOSER SHOT WE SEE Collins and Curtis. Collins is a big man, rough and hearty, clearly a leader. He was a saloon keeper and brawler before the war and even a prison diet has not shrunk his waist (of course, as will be seen, he eats far better than other prisoners). He is brilliantly, outlandishly dressed, sleek, in a fancy long green coat and waistcoat, a Peacock among endless paupers, and he has a raucous good humor about him, a larger-than-life quality.

He roars amiably to Munn—

> COLLINS
> Let the fish go—we'll roast 'em another time!

Curtis, his partner-in-crime, not as big, is cold as the grave. There is not an ounce of humor in him but rather a grim sense of purpose. He, too, is a leader of the men around them.

> CURTIS
> Don't waste your time with that bunch. Come back
> with your pards.

> COLLINS
> And you know who they are, don'tcha, Mick?!

—so discretion plus that message tells Munn to back off. Snarling at Dick . . .

> MUNN
> We'll take care of you later.

. . . and with as much bluff as he can muster he saunters back to his friends, leaving Dick to explain to the still-wondering Josiah and the others . . .

> DICK
> Call 'em 'Raiders'—hyenas is more like it. One of 'em
> steers the new boys over to the rest where they hit
> you over the head, kill you even—steal your goods
> for themselves.

Can that be true? Josiah and McSpadden look to the other Old Prisoners, who confirm that it is.

> MCSPADDEN
> Why doesn't someone stop 'em!

Some of the Old Prisoners are embarrassed and shame-faced, some defensive and angry.

> OLD PRISONER #1
> They run the place.

> MCSPADDEN
> What do you mean, they run the place! What do the Rebs (in the towers there) do? Why don't they stop 'em??

> OLD PRISONER #1
> Stop 'em? They *trade* with 'em—give 'em food—whiskey—anything they want—

> OLD PRISONER #2
> Took 7th Vermont's coats, blankets, rations, *shoes*! Cold nights then—didn't have a chance—didn't last a week.

> MCSPADDEN
> *(can't believe it . . .)*
> And they're on our side, y'say?

> OLD PRISONER #2
> *(contemptuously)*
> Bounty jumpers. Crawled out of the gutters of New York or wherever for the joining-up money—all they meant to do was run away 'fore they saw any fighting—

Med. Long on Munn

As he rejoins Curtis and Collins. They all look at the New Group with menace and then Collins says something with which the others agree.

> JOSIAH
> *(to Dick)*
> Then we're very much obliged to you, friend.

> DICK
> Friend? . . .
> *(puzzled)*
> Do you not know me? . . .
> *(no . . . should we . . . ?)*
> Sergeant? . . . Josiah? . . .

Josiah and his Friends look at each other, genuinely confused. Dick is devastated.

> DICK
> Old *Dick* only joined up with you! Old *Dick* only fit with you at Seven Pines and the Chickahominy, at Antietam and—

> JOSIAH
> Dick . . . *Potter*? Is that you?

> DICK
> *(bitterly)*
> Well it's no wonder, is it! No food to eat . . . ! No clothes to wear . . . ! No way to see how bad I look. . . !

> JOSIAH
> Dick?! We thought you were killed two years ago—

Now Dick's astonished and delighted friends cluster closely around him, trying to make it up, to console him . . . We weren't expecting to see you here is all . . . We thought you was killed at Antietam . . . Lord, Dick, we'd given you up two years ago . . . You look fine, Dick! . . . Handsome as you ever were . . . !

And they do it well enough, in time, to make amends, to mollify him, even to cheer him up, sort of. . . .

DICK

Weren't killed at all. Shot in both legs is all. . . .
(grins to Josiah)
Surprised to see me, huh, Josie!

JOSIAH
(touched)
When are we going fishing again?
(to the Old Prisoners)
Dick and his father are the best fishermen in New Bedford.

DICK

And that's saying a lot.

But McSpadden's look to Josiah says he's shocked to the core.

TUCKER
(anxiously)
Tell us what sort of place we're in, Dick.

As they all wait for his answer, which will be an inexpressibly bitter one—you want to know what sort of place this is, do you?. . . .

New Angle Featuring Wirz at the Main Gate

. . . Wirz comes in, accompanied by a dozen guards on foot, including the dreaded, red-haired LT. BARRETT. Wirz looks at the new men critically . . . and then at the Old Prisoners around them. His right hand pains him as usual and he flexes it as—

WIRZ
So—I ask you again—where is my bridle and halter?

No one answers him, not the Prisoners already standing there or those coming over to hear what Wirz is saying, so . . .

WIRZ
What, you don't care, no rations today unless the god-dam thief returns what he stole from me?

From the Old Prisoners a GRUMBLE of anger, hatred . . . Why you punishing us, you damned Dutchman? . . . You goddam Wirz, we didn't do it . . . that Wirz ignores. He looks at the men digging wells. . . .

> WIRZ
> If those are wells for drinking water, I say all right . . . tunnels, you will suffer the consequences.
> *(he looks at Josiah and McSpadden*
> *and the other new men)*
> Tunnels are useless. Even if you are outside I give any two men a twelve hour start and then track you with dogs—and you suffer the consequences.
> *(then, changing keys—)*
> But why bother anyway? I know absolutely there are talks going on this moment for Exchange. Any day you will all be paroled, in quick order . . .
> *(then—)*
> So. We understand each other. No bridle, no halter, no rations. . . .

The Old Prisoners start to curse and surge forward.

> OLD PRISONERS
> You damn Wirz . . . damn you . . .

They aren't close enough to be really dangerous but Wirz, frightened, starts to back up. He pulls his revolver and makes his way out, quickly moving backwards—

Med. Shot on Lt. Barrett

At the head of the Guards, interposing himself between the retreating Wirz and the advancing Prisoners. He no more than aims his pistol at the advancing prisoners when—

His POV of the Advancing Prisoners

—they mutter and slow to a stop. This is a man to be afraid of.

Full Shot Includes Barrett

> LT. BARRETT
> Go on about your own business now, you know
> what's good for you.

And reluctantly they do.

On Dick, Josiah, McSpadden

Watching Wirz go. Dick is one of the men looking in contempt after
Wirz.

> DICK
> Wirz is nothing but a damn liar. You hear anything
> about any Exchange for us?
> *(no)*
> Always tells new men there's about to be an Exchange
> so they won't try to run off.

> JOSIAH
> You haven't eaten today?

> DICK
> *(snorts)*
> Yesterday neither—Somebody stole a bridle off a
> carthorse so Wirz's punishing the whole camp.

Touched, Josiah takes something out of his pocket, gives it to Dick,
whose eyes go wide . . .

> DICK
> What's that—
> *(a whisper)*
> —*salt pork*? I ain't seen salt pork since I been here.

> JOSIAH
> Rebs gave it to us 'fore they put us on the train.

A Confederate sentinel in a Turkey Roost.

DICK
(snorts, disbelieving)

Rebs!

Josiah presses the pork on him. Really? You sure. God bless you, Josie. You really sure . . . ? You may want this yourself . . . But even as Josiah motions to go ahead, Dick's already devouring the meat, gnawing, tearing at it with his teeth.

TUCKER
(nervously)
Ain't you gonna wait to fry it up, Dick?

DICK

No wood.

(tearing away . . .)

Got no wood for a fire.

[41]

SWEET
Have this here onion, Dick.

DICK
An onion! Forgot what an onion tastes like. . . .

And he grabs and devours that too, in great tearing bites, as the other old prisoners look on enviously and desperately and Josiah and McSpadden and their friends wonder what on God's earth they got into.

Dick finishes the onion and gives a loud, satisfied belch.

DICK
Meal fit for a king . . . Well boys—would you care to look around now, see your new home? . . . Let's see . . . What'cha want to see first?

JOSIAH
Is there a surgeon here, Dick, to look at the Sergeant? Got a bullet in his shoulder.

Dick snorts, shakes his head contemptuously. He tosses a look of dismissal at—

Sick Call

. . . A long line of a hundred men or more, most looking a lot worse than McSpadden, most lying (a few standing) in the sand, waiting to see one over-worked but not overly involved Doctor. The line is not moving.

Back to Scene

DICK
Sick call. Do nothin' for you.

MCSPADDEN
I'm fine. Show us around, Dick.

He isn't fine, and everyone knows, but they all exchange a look that
says there's nothing to do about it, so—

DICK
Let's see—over there—

He looks, points to—

To Include Men in Ball-and-Chain, Seen from Our Group's POV

—half-a-dozen men all chained to one large 36-pound ball so none
can move unless all move together.

Back to Scene

DICK
Caught those boys trying to escape.

MCSPADDEN
How long they been in that thing?

DICK
(forever . . .)
Since the day they caught 'em.
(. . . of course)
Let's see . . .
(what else should I show you?)
I know.
(to Josiah, cheerfully)
I'll show you were we *ain't* going fishing. . . .

He starts to stump off toward the Swamp. Before the men follow, they
exchange a look of shock.

The Swamp

Our group stands and looks into the Swamp . . .

. . . with men drinking from it, bathing in it, doing other things as well.

SOUND: There is now, and whenever we are at the Swamp, the angry hum of swarming flies.

The new men wave and slash the air around them, trying to chase the flies. The old men like Dick . . . less so.

> DICK
> What they did! What they did was build this whole place downstream from their tents and horses and dogs and everything—so they do whatever they do into the water 'fore it even comes here—and you're not seeing the tenth of what we do to it—so a man with any sense'd die rather'n drink from it.

> 2ND WISCONSIN
> That's the only water there is . . . ?

> DICK
> Some boys and I are planning on digging a well up there—
> *(his voice drops)*
> —two, really. One for drinking, one for getting away—want to see?

Damn right they do, and the sooner the better. All are depressed, none more than Sweet, who is still looking at the Swamp.

> SWEET
> They do *everything* in there?
> *(when Dick shrugs as if to say—*
> *Who's to stop 'em?)*
> That's why this whole place has such a stink to it?

> DICK
> You won't notice it so much after a couple of months.
> C'mon . . . some pards I want you to meet.

As they go, Sweet confides in Josiah, privately, not wanting to hurt Dick's feelings . . .

> SWEET
> Won't notice it? My pigsty back home don't smell bad
> as that. . . .

. . . and they pass a Swamp-side Laundry and a Tailor advertising their services for hire. McSpadden staggers from his shoulder wound, then catches himself with Billy's help and turns to Tucker—

> McSPADDEN
> You got all your tailorin' things with you, Tuck?
> Shears and thread and such?
> *(yes, so to all . . .)*
> One of us is going to be all right in here. One of us is
> going to be *rich*!

A little laughter among them, shared by Tucker most of all, as they go off.

> DICK
> And we'll enter old Sweet here in the prizefights. . . .

As they move off, maybe fifty yards away a little drama is being played out. They SEE and as they keep walking a couple of them, feeling better, are even a little amused by . . .

At the Deadline

A cheery Young Prisoner, ETHAN, one of a group at the Deadline, is good-naturedly calling up to a VERY YOUNG (14-year-old) GUARD in a Tower who is next to a VERY YOUNG GUARD #2. Both guards have .69 calibre smoothbore flintlock muskets.

> ETHAN
> Hey, Johnny—Hey, Secesh—Hey, sonny—you got
> something to eat?

YOUNG GUARD
Yeah, I got something to eat.

ETHAN
What'cha got?

YOUNG GUARD
Got two ears of corn.

ETHAN
Give you a dollar for 'em.
(holding it up)
A Yankee greenback for both ears.

The two Young Guards confer privately. They look down at Ethan and perhaps there is a sense that they are not pleased at having been called 'Johnny' and 'Secesh.' They whisper—discuss it with some little excitement—and then Young Guard calls down . . .

YOUNG GUARD
You come over here.

ETHAN
Not me. I ain't coming over there.

Our Group   Featuring Josiah, Dick

Watching. Some of them are amused at the by-play, but not Dick Potter. He shakes his head grimly to Josiah and McSpadden—this could be bad. Josiah looks back uncertainly, not understanding why.

Med. Shot on Lt. Barrett

Watching from another Turkey Roost. Barrett never takes his eyes from the scene at the Deadline.

[46]

Back to the Young Guard and Ethan

> YOUNG GUARD
> Why not?

> ETHAN
> 'Cause it's the Deadline. You'll shoot me if I do.

> YOUNG GUARD #2
> Who says he will?

> You want something or not?

> ETHAN
> Yeah. I want two ears of corn.

> YOUNG GUARD
> Then step across.
> *(shows an ear of corn, takes a tiny nibble)*
> Won't last long if'n you don't.

Ethan, terrifically tempted, turns to his friends, grins in the playful spirit of the moment. Whaddya think? Should I?

Some call—

Our Group

> DICK
> *(calling)*
> He's a Reb, ain't he? Don't trust him.

Dick standing next to Josiah and McSpadden and Billy, all watching tensely—

> JOSIAH
> He's just a little boy up there, Dick—

> DICK
> Rebs are running out of men. Robbing the cradle and
> grave to guard us.

[47]

McSPADDEN
Is he playing a game with him?

DICK
(no)
These kiddies scare me worse'n soldiers . . . Say they
get a 30-day furlough when they shoot one of us.

At Josiah's sharp, questioning look—

DICK
(Ethan) Must be new here—

Close on Lt. Barrett in a Turkey Roost

Watching closely, keeping his distance, not interfering—though he has
the power to do whatever he wants here.

Resume Ethan

He has a cheerful answer for each of his friends.

ETHAN
He ain't gonna shoot me . . . He's just a pup . . . He
wants the dollar. Probably never had one.
(Don't do it, Ethan)
Yeah, but I sure do want that corn. Can't you just
taste it?

Intercutting

YOUNG GUARD
(another nibble)
Better hurry then. . . .

Our cheery Ethan hesitates.

The Moment of Truth.

He grins and sticks a toe almost to the Deadline.

[48]

His friends, those who are standing next to him, are worried. A couple back away a foot or two, muttering.

Mad Matthew hops around gleefully and claps his hands.

Our Group exchanges looks.

The Young Guard takes another tiny nibble. He waves the corn.

> YOUNG GUARD
> Goin' fast.

With a bold final grin and a look and shrug at his friends—What the hell?—Ethan calls up . . .

> ETHAN
> All right. Here I come. . . .

. . . and ducks under the Deadline rail . . .

. . . and is immediately SHOT by the Young Guard.

As Our Group jumps in horror . . .

. . . and Ethan flops and gasps, shot through the throat, his blood and life spurting away . . .

. . . and his enraged friends rise up and shout and wave their fists at The Tower . . .

. . . and others of Ethan's horrified friends drag him back across the Deadline, joined by Mad Matthew who doesn't understand but knows it's exciting . . .

. . . and the Young Guard quickly, excitedly, reloads.

> YOUNG GUARD #2
> (to the Prisoners)
> He warned him! He warned him!

. . . as the Guards in the other Towers hold their muskets ready . . .

. . . and Ethan dies his bloody death.

His friend, galvanized, shouts his rage . . .

> OLD PRISONER
> Oh, give the little son-of-a-bitch a thirty day furlough
> . . . Dirty little coward . . .

Lt. Barrett in the Far Turkey Roost

> LT. BARRETT
> *(calling)*
> You know the rules.
>
> You all know the rules.

Old Prisoners

Still protesting bitterly . . .

> OLD PRISONER
> Thirty day furlough—what a Reb won't do!

Med. on Our Group

Dick is bitter. Everyone else is shocked and disbelieving, Billy perhaps most of all. They look from Dick to Josiah and McSpadden and back to the scene. My God.

> SWEET
> What do they do, Dick? Shoot you for fun in here?

It seems so. Indeed it does. HOLD.

Fade Out.

Fade In:

Ext.   Outside the Star Fort — Day

Two Confederate Officers, COL. CHANDLER and LT. DAHLGREN, ride on horseback past The Dead House on their way to the Star Fort. They look uncommonly interested in what they pass—

—The Stocks (empty now) and Very Young Guards and the cannon pointing into The Stockade. They dismount and enter—

Ext.   Star Fort — Day

—and make their way to Wirz's quarters. A sentry steps quickly out of the way to let them in.

Int.   Wirz's Headquarters — Day

Colonel Chandler comes up to Wirz, who is writing at his table. Wirz is surprised to see him.

> CHANDLER
> Captain Wirz? . . . 'Morning, Captain. I'm Colonel Chandler. This is my aide, Lt. Dahlgren . . . The Department of War has detailed me to inspect all our prison camps—
> *(giving Wirz his credentials)*
> We'll try not to create any fuss, 'though we may be here a while—

> WIRZ
> Yes, of course. If there is anyth—

> CHANDLER
> No—You just proceed with your duties. If I need to speak with you, I'm sure I'll be able to find you. Thank you, Captain. . . .

He salutes—Wirz salutes—Yes, sir—thank you, sir—and Chandler and Dahlgren exit. Wirz clearly is not happy about this. . . .

[51]

Ext.   Full Shot Inside the Stockade — Day

CAMERA PANS The Stockade, where all is quiet. We come to Dick
Potter's open-air, partly-covered 'Shebang' . . . one which has just a
little room around it where McSpadden and Josiah and Our Group
will shortly make their own Shebang . . .

Ext.   Dick Potter's Shebang — Day

. . . and where now Tucker is tenderly cutting Dick Potter's hair as the
rest of the Massachusetts men get as comfortable as they can. . . .

> DICK
> *(to Tucker)*
> You're taking five pounds of hair and ten pounds of
> bugs off me—

. . . while a few feet away, facing them, is the 184th Pennsylvania Shebang. JOHN GLEASON, their Sergeant and leader, strong and lean,
is standing outside it, looking around, almost as if on watch . . .

. . . as fifty yards away . . .

A Confederate Tunnel Gang

. . . is poking in the ground near a Shebang with long sticks and ax-
handles. The 'gang'—three soldiers, seven slaves—is looking here,
poking there, when suddenly—

—the ground outside a Shebang gives way and the Confederate Soldiers call 'Tunnel! Tunnel!' . . . and a tremendous commotion starts.
The Confederate Guards grab a protesting IOWA PRIVATE, start to
hustle him off in the direction of the Pennsylvania Shebang, where . . .

WE SEE MARTIN BLACKBURN, second-in-command of the Pennsylvania men, a man of good and gentle character who has been watching the Confederate Gang at work. He detaches himself and quickly—

not so quickly as to call attention to himself—comes back to the Pennsylvania Shebang to whisper privately to Gleason—

> BLACKBURN
> Found the Iowa Tunnel. Headin' this way . . .

Gleason immediately ducks into the Pennsylvania Shebang—

—all this is observed by McSpadden and the Massachusetts men, who also see the Confederate Soldiers hustling the Iowa Private past them, paying no attention to his cries . . .

> IOWA PRIVATE
> It's a well!, it's a well!

. . . and off they go. McSpadden has seen it all. He looks at the disappearing Confederates and then to the Pennsylvania Shebang where Gleason has disappeared. He turns to Dick Potter.

> McSPADDEN
> Dick? . . . These the boys you say are digging the tunnel?

> DICK
> *(hesitates)*
> You're my Sergeant but . . . some questions it's hard to ask in here. . . .

> McSPADDEN
> *(a moment—)*
> Go tell that Sergeant I'd be grateful for a private word with him—that we mean no harm and he can trust us.

Dick nods and goes to the Pennsylvania Shebang. All quiet, all observed by all the Massachusetts men. They wait expectantly until—

—Gleason comes out with Dick Potter. He looks at McSpadden critically, skeptically, and then motions to him to—

—follow me, over here, alone. They go off, and when they are alone, very privately—

> McSPADDEN
> I don't want to do anything against the grain here, Sergeant—we mean you no harm—Dick Potter there will vouch for us—I've got some good men here who'll do anything they can to get out of this place— if there's any way we could be of some help to you . . .

DURING THIS, as McSpadden and Gleason have walked away, all the Massachusetts men are watching, praying that this deal will be made. They also look at—

—Two Pennsylvania men, TOBIAS, an irrepressible teen-ager, and BENTON, his older friend. Both sides are sizing each other up, seeing if this would be a marriage to make. The Pennsylvania men, too, watch—

—McSpadden make his case to Gleason. Gleason studies him, studies the other Massachusetts men, listens, listens—

—as out of the Pennsylvania Shebang comes WISNOVSKY, a hard man who has clearly just been digging in the dirt.

Finally Gleason makes up his mind. To McSpadden—

> GLEASON
> Get your men.

And follow me. They do, all eagerly going into the Pennsylvania Shebang.

Inside the Pennsylvania Shebang

All the Pennsylvania men . . . all the Massachusetts men . . . crowded in, anxious to hear. McSpadden, shifting position because of the pain in his shoulder, is saying to his men—

MCSPADDEN

(I told him) 'course we'll help with the digging, and glad for the chance.

GLEASON

Got tools?

MCSPADDEN

Boys?

The group looks momentarily defeated.

DICK

Spoons. Pans. Canteens. Anything.

Oh, sure we've got tools. Josiah and the others—all except the unfriendly and cautious Tyce—eagerly fish through their haversacks, come up with an assortment, mostly canteens which they break in half for two digging implements. The Pennsylvania men are pleased.

NOTE: Gleason, their leader, wears the one good uniform among the Pennsylvania men, a blue jacket with three brass buttons. Young Tobias is now and always barefoot.

JOSIAH

We don't want to do anything hurts your chances. If we'd be a problem to you . . .

GLEASON

More of us they have to follow, better the chances some of us making it.

MCSPADDEN

What's chances of getting outside the walls?

BLACKBURN

We know a thing or two about tunnelin'.

DICK

These boys—

- (MORE) -

DICK (cont.)
(Gleason, Martin Blackburn, Wisnovsky)
—are all coal miners from West Pennsylvania.

McSpadden and Josiah exchange a look: This is hopeful!

TUCKER
And once we get outside?

DICK
They heard Wirz talkin' 'bout his dogs.

McSPADDEN
(with meaning)
We *saw* the dogs.

TOBIAS
We got a nice surprise for old Wirz.
(to Gleason)
Can I tell?

GLEASON
One of their slaves they got working on the wall
brung us a map. We can go creek and river the whole
way—swim and float on logs—creeks to Flint
River—Flint to Appalachicola—Appalachicola to the
Gulf of Mexico.

TOBIAS
Ain't a dog alive can follow us if we never touch land.

All the other new men take hope. This is thrilling news.

McSPADDEN
When can we start with the digging?

GLEASON
Soon as you eat in the morning.

WISNOVSKY
If you eat.

BLACKBURN
Hard work. Need to keep your strength up.

McSPADDEN
How long will the diggin' take?

GLEASON
Month. Maybe more, maybe less . . .

Josiah looks to his Group—and then dumps his haversack on the ground. His friends all agree with what he's doing, all except Tyce, as—

JOSIAH
All we have is a little hardtack but you're welcome to
half of it.

Josiah and the others hand bits of food around to their new friends, who take it gratefully and divide it into equal shares before they start to eat.

DICK
(declines the food)
I already had mine.

He belches.

McSpadden isn't feeling well. Even though he's sitting down, he seems to lose his balance. He falls to one side.

JOSIAH
(taking charge)
Let's give him some room. Massachusetts men—
wait outside.

They go.

GLEASON
Pennsylvania men too.
- (MORE) -

[57]

GLEASON (cont.)
(all except . . .)
Martin. You stay.

After the others go, they look at the now-unconscious McSpadden.
Then . . .

GLEASON
All we got's a pocket knife.

JOSIAH
You ever do anything like that?

No. And Josiah's look, when Gleason looks to him with the same question, says Neither have I. And neither has Martin. But . . .

JOSIAH
I don't see as we have a choice.

They agree. HOLD.

Inside the Shebang — Close on McSpadden — Night

McSpadden, now conscious, lying on his back. Gleason says to him—

GLEASON
Wish I had some whiskey (for you) . . . .

MCSPADDEN
I always wish I had some whiskey.

He jams a dirty cloth in his own mouth, bites down hard, nods to
them: go ahead.

Gleason wipes the knife on his pants the best he can . . . Martin Blackburn washes McSpadden's shoulder ('It's rainwater, Sergeant') and
then, with Josiah, holds McSpadden down and Gleason starts to dig
for the bullet.

When he can't bear it any more McSpadden passes out. His head lolls to the side.

Gleason glances at Josiah, who nods: keep going.

Gleason does.

Ext. The Prison — Night

OPEN ON THE GUARDS in the Turkey Roosts, framed against the moon. Now . . .

. . . THE CAMERA ROVES DOWN AND ACROSS the whole prison, and WE HEAR, coming from the Den of the Raiders, AND SEE DIS-TANTLY . . .

. . . a drunken, noisy, brightly-torch-lit, riotous island of men, no more than a few hundred in this sea of thousands, and they are SINGING bawdy chanteys, led by the enormous green-coated Collins, weaving drunkenly against the sky with not a care in the world . . .

. . . and OVER THIS, FARAWAY at first . . .

DICK POTTER'S VOICE
Whiskey . . . Need some whiskey . . .

. . . and now we SEE Dick Potter, swinging along on his crutches, walking with Josiah. Josiah is holding his spare shirt. They are maybe fifty yards from the Raiders, picking their way through sleeping and talking men, and Dick is calling . . .

DICK
Need some whiskey . . . got a shirt to trade . . . Need some whiskey for a Sergeant. . . .

JOSIAH
(to Dick alone . . .)
Doesn't have to be whiskey. Rather have medicine. . . .

Dick gives him a look as he stumps along: the look says 'Whiskey'll be hard enough to find in this place, but medicine? in here??' . . . and as they pass SAMSON, an older, one-legged prisoner, a firebrand, and LIMBER JIM, a strong young frontiersman. . . .

DICK

New man here. Needs whiskey. Got a shirt to trade . . .

SAMSON
(gestures bitterly)
They got whiskey up there—Raiders got whiskey— (But if you) go up there, (you'll) come back without your shirt, without your whiskey, without one of your legs—if you're lucky. . . .

LIMBER JIM
(looks at the Raiders)
We'll have our day—

DICK
(not interested)
New man here. Got a shirt, good shirt to trade . . .

HUB

Give you a piece of wood . . .

Dick doesn't think that's such a bad offer . . . HUB is holding up a limb of rough pine that's maybe two feet long . . . but Josiah doesn't want it . . .

JOSIAH

No—thank you anyway . . .

. . . when from nowhere PATRICK SHAY, not quite 16 years old, the jaunty, beloved unofficial (but real) mascot of Andersonville, falls in beside them. Survivors say he kept spirits up wherever he went in Andersonville . . . as he does tonight . . .

Dick Potter (portrayed by Gregory Sporleder) introduces Josiah Day, at the right, to the little drummer boy Patrick Shay (Blake Heron). Shay, a real prisoner at Andersonville, was a drummer with the 61st New York. At age 15, he was called the "oldest man in Andersonville" because he was one of the first captured.

PATRICK
Got a good shirt here . . . need some good whiskey for a good Sergeant . . . good shirt, good man, need some good whiskey . . .

DICK
(to Josiah)
Patrick . . . New York Drummer Boy . . . catched at Culpepper . . . been here since they built it . . . call him the oldest man here. . . .

He grins at Josiah and as they go off in one direction and Patrick in another . . .

. . . CAMERA PULLS UP AND AWAY and as we HEAR Dick and Patrick still calling 'Shirt for whiskey . . . shirt for medicine . . . shirt to trade . . .' CAMERA REVEALS men sleeping on the ground or try-

[61]

ing to, some naked or near, some shivering, some clinging to each other spoon-like for warmth, two or three fevered and thrashing . . . and OVER ALL THIS, CROSS-FADE JOSIAH'S VOICE OVER Dick's . . .

JOSIAH'S VOICE OVER
Dear Mother and Father . . .

I am writing you from my new home, in Andersonville Prison, in Georgia. We arrived here after a long and not very comfortable ride by railroad. I am with my Sergeant and Thomas Sweet and Elijah Tucker and some of the others and we are mostly all well. . . We did find the most wonderful thing when we got here. Dick Potter is alive and was not killed as we all thought. He has been here a long time and is 'showing us the ropes,' as we say. He was wounded in both legs but is better now. We are going fishing with his father as soon as we come home and then I want him to visit with us, mother, so you can fatten him up with your butter biscuits and mince pie. . . .

DURING THE END OF THE ABOVE, WE HEAR a solo banjo playing a reprise of 'Kathleen Mavoureen' and the CAMERA BRINGS US BACK TO:

The Pennsylvania Shebang — Night

—where Martin Blackburn is playing the banjo and singing quietly. All the Massachusetts and Pennsylvania men are listening, but Martin sees Thomas Sweet is listening particularly raptly so . . .

BLACKBURN
You like music. I can tell . . . You play anything?

SWEET
Wish I did.

BLACKBURN
C'mere. Sit by me. I'll teach you.

[62]

You will?

And as Martin makes room for him and starts to show him the fingering. . . .

Inside Dick Potter's Shebang — Night

McSpadden is on the ground, shivering in his uncomfortable sleep, an extra shirt wrapped around him, not having an easy time of it.

Billy, next to him, watching him closely, is stripped to the waist.

Josiah and Dick Potter enter the Shebang and stand above them, looking down, concerned.

JOSIAH
How is he?

BILLY
Feverish.

JOSIAH
That your shirt (around him)?
(yes)
Put this one around him too.

He gives Billy his spare shirt and Billy does. Then—

JOSIAH
You want to be relieved?

BILLY
(no)
I'm all right.
(by way of apology . . .)
Just knowing we're going to get out of here . . .
(to Dick, with a nod . . .)
Coal miners.

That's all right. That's pretty good. Josiah nods—'Night, Billy—and he and Dick exit.

Outside the Shebang

Josiah comes out of the Shebang with Dick, gets pencil and paper from his haversack and settles down to write. Dick lies on the ground next to him—

DICK

Writing home, Josie?
(yes . . .)
Give 'em my respects, would you?

JOSIAH

I will.
(then—)
(You're) bald as a new-hatched egg, Dick.

DISTANT VOICE #1

Egg? Egg?? Give you ten dollar for it.

Faraway, a man laughs.

DICK

Must've had a thousand chiggers in my hair—itched like the devil.

TUCKER'S VOICE
(ten yards away . . .)

Friend—when they do feed you around here—what is it they feed you?

VOICE #2

Mush.

TUCKER

Mush?

VOICES #2,3,4,5,6

Mush!

[64]

VOICE #2

Rotten cornmeal mush.

A little snort, almost nervous laughter, from Tucker. Dick turns to Josiah . . .

DICK

Josiah? . . . Tell me about the boys.

JOSIAH

We're way down. From 100 to 42, last I know.

DICK

Cousin Bob?

JOSIAH

Killed at Cold Harbor. Benjamin and James, too.
(then—)
Can I get a letter out of here?

DICK

If you give a Guard two dollars. You got two dollars?
(no)
I got one squirreled away. I'll give you it but one ain't enough.
(turns anxiously . . .)
Josie? . . . You think my father knows I'm a prisoner?
If you all thought I was killed . . .
(Josie doesn't know)
I would'a wrote him but I didn't have the money either . . .
(then—)
Be terrible, he thinks I'm dead.

JOSIAH

Just think when you show up alive and kicking . . .

DICK

Well, I don't know about the kicking.

He lifts his crutch, smiles a broad smile. In the Silence . . .

Med. Shot on Blackburn, Sweet

As Blackburn shows Sweet the fingering on the banjo . . .

> BLACKBURN
> Tomorrow, if you boys want, we'll take you grey-
> back racing.

> SWEET
> Greybacks?

> BLACKBURN
> That's what we call the lice in here. We race 'em . . .
> bet on 'em. . . .

> SWEET
> We call Johnny Reb 'greyback.'

> BLACKBURN
> Well in here, we call lice greybacks and Johnny Reb
> lice.

Laughter from the men.

We become dimly aware that in the far background the Raiders'
drunken chanteys have died out.

Resume Josiah, Dick Potter

CAMERA HOLDS Josiah and Dick foreground as Blackburn and
Sweet play banjo in the background. Quietly, privately . . .

> DICK
> The way you kill the lice in here, Josie—get some
> wood, hold your clothes close as you can to the fire
> without them catching and they'll go pop-pop-pop
> . . . Flies and chiggers and gnats and things—
> - (MORE) -

[66]

DICK (cont.)
(waving, swatting)
—can't do anything about them. They get you even
at night.

JOSIAH
Dick? Why do they keep officers separate from the
men? Is it like they say—they don't want the men to
have their leaders?

DICK
Have a few anyway. Got two captains from the 54th
Massachusetts—they're punishing 'em for leading
colored troops by putting 'em here—
(that's a fact)
Don't really need officers. Never saw the day a plain
New Bedford fisherman couldn't out-fight, out-think,
out-anything a Johnny Reb.

60TH OHIO'S VOICE
What do you do when it rains here?

DISTANT VOICE #1
Git wet, you dern fool.

More distant laughter. Back to Dick and Josiah . . .

DICK
You catch it. Catch the rain in your clothes and wring
'em out and drink it. Don't drink from the Swamp.
You'll get sick. You'll die.

JOSIAH
What do you do when it doesn't rain?

DICK
Do without.

JOSIAH
You do? How?

[67]

DICK

You gotta teach yourself.
(then —)
I get a swallow from a well every now and then . . .
You can do it, Josie. Lotta the boys can't but you can.

Dick looks up—Josiah, too—as little Patrick has again materialized.
He is holding out a broken bottle half full of whiskey to Josiah—

PATRICK

For your Sergeant.

Josiah, surprised, takes the bottle—Dick is unsurprised, and grins as
Josiah smells it. That's good whiskey!

JOSIAH

I don't know where you got this but—wait a minute—let me get the shirt. I gave it to the Serg . . .

He gets up—but Patrick is already gone. Dick makes a generous gesture: That's Patrick for you.

Touched, Josiah takes the open bottle the couple of feet to . . .

Int.   Dick Potter's Shebang — Night

. . . and enters. McSpadden is still feverish, Billy still trying to keep him
comfortable. Josiah watches silently. Then—

JOSIAH

Give him a taste of this when he wakes up.

Sure you don't want to be relieved?

I'm fine. Josiah nods, exits.

[68]

Ext. Shebang — Night

As Josiah rejoins Dick. He looks around at this new world before . . .

> JOSIAH
> Will you show us what else we have to do, Dick? to
> stay alive in this place?

> DICK
> *(yes)*
> We really will go fishing together, won't we, soon as
> we get out of here? I've been looking forward to that
> more'n anything.
>
> Of all my friends, my father always liked you and
> Bob best.
>
> Me, too.

Josiah is touched as . . .

> VOICE
> RAIDERS! RAIDERS!

Martin Blackburn's BANJO STOPS discordantly in mid-chord as instantly the men are alert and on their feet—but already fifty Raiders are upon them, with clubs and knives and rocks.

We SEE Collins and Curtis leading the assault.

> COLLINS
> Now boys! Get everything they've got.

They wave their men in. Collins, huge and resplendent, lays about him with a club, knocking men over left and right. Maybe he and his men aren't quite as drunk as they earlier let on. Munn and Curtis and their henchmen attack Dick and the new men, trying to hurt them as much as to get their goods, smashing into them with fists and heavy weapons.

In Dick Potter's Shebang

McSpadden blinks awake in this nightmare. As the Shebang is trampled he struggles helplessly to get off the ground but, despite everything Billy does to try to protect him, he is, they both are, trampled by the Raiders.

Ext.   Around the Shebang

Munn dances around, waving his knife, giving directions, but is careful to stay out of danger himself.

Dick and his friends, Josiah and his group, Tyce and 60th Ohio, fight back desperately in the dark with Sweet, the quiet giant, doing fierce work in his and Martin Blackburn's defense . . .

. . . and with Dick, having his crutch ripped away by Curtis, now in a hand-to-hand fight . . .

. . . as Munn, dancing and waving his knife, points out Dick and calls . . .

MUNN
That's him. Get him, get him!

And WE SEE IN CLOSE-UP Collins swing at Dick with his club but we do NOT SEE the result, which is lost in the general maelstrom as . . .

. . . Munn, seeing Dick's back is now to him, runs toward him with his knife up . . .

GLEASON
Fight, boys! For your lives!

. . . Gleason is strong and capable and leads the defense as WE SEE shadows, images, flashing knives and swinging clubs, and bodies going down . . .

. . . Wisnovsky, the coal miner, fighting back hard . . .

. . . Josiah, too . . .

. . . and WE SEE CLOSE UP McSpadden still struggling and Billy still trying to cover him but McSpadden shaking him off to get up, only to be hit in the face with a heavy club BY CURTIS and going down, clutching his face and eyes . . .

. . . and the Raiders take their booty—Josiah's haversack, Tucker's, Martin Blackburn's banjo, utensils—and march off.

. . . and the men are left bloody and hard-breathing to look at the damage.

> TUCKER
> My shears! My thread!

> GLEASON
> Anybody hurt?. . . .

> 2ND WISCONSIN
> My coat! My blanket! They got my coat and blanket!

Moving with Curtis, Collins, Other Raiders

Walking—almost marching—not running away. Collins is holding up a coat and blanket in triumph and roaring—

> COLLINS
> Stick with Collins, boys, you'll live like Kings!

Curtis, with Munn at his side, has two haversacks. Munn, holding tight to Martin Blackburn's banjo, looks back angrily over his shoulder, almost daring them to come after him.

Close on McSpadden

Struggling up. Blood streams down his face, into his eyes.

> MCSPADDEN
> Massachusetts men! Everybody all right?

Full Shot

The men look around at each other in the moonlight, stunned by the ferocity of what they've just been through.

Martin Blackburn forlornly mourns his lost banjo. To Sweet . . .

> BLACKBURN
> My music . . .

Sweet puts a comforting hand on his shoulder.

> SWEET
> We'll get it back.

Close on McSpadden

Dazed, bloody, spinning, looking . . .

> MCSPADDEN
> Josie, lad? Where are you? You all right?

Josiah

Josiah is kneeling down. He is silently cradling Dick in his arms, and Dick is dead. Josiah looks up at the blood-spattered McSpadden.

Hold this *Pieta* into . . .

Fade Out.

Fade In:

Ext.   The Dead House Outside the Walls — Day

Josiah and Tobias come out of the Dead House and, under guard, return to The Stockade. As they come, they pass a wagon arriving with dead bodies. Josiah stops and looks at it while Tobias points to a couple of large, heavy pieces of wood on the ground and says to his guard—

> TOBIAS
> All right?

The Guard shrugs—Yeah, you can have that. Tobias picks it up and they go back to The Stockade.

Inside The Stockade — Day

Sergeant Gleason is one of the group of Sergeants at the horse-drawn food wagon just inside the gate. He is waiting for the small sack of food for his full mess and looking at—

—Col. Chandler, the Confederacy's Inspector, and Lt. Dahlgren, who are walking around the prison, looking at everything and everyone. Chandler speaks privately to Dahlgren, who makes notes as—

At the Main Gate — Day

Josiah and Tobias return from outside the prison. They come to Gleason, who looks away from Col. Chandler to ask them—

> GLEASON
> (Been) Taking Dick to the Dead House?

Josiah nods bleakly. Tobias sees the Prisoners looking at Chandler and Dahlgren, asks—

> TOBIAS
> Who's that?

> GLEASON
> Some Rebs the Government sent down to inspect us.

Nice to know they care.

Josiah looks at Chandler and then, without visibly sharing Gleason's bitterness, leaves to return to Our Group. Tobias stays to show Gleason the pieces of wood.

> TOBIAS
>
> Look what I found on the way back from the Dead House. We can have a fire—make bread, dumplings, anything we want.

Tobias is young and he's been here a long time and seen too much to be affected by one more Death. Gleason takes a small burlap sack of meal from the guards.

> GLEASON
>
> Boys'll vote on it.

They start back toward the Group.

Our Group at the Remnants of Dick Potter's Shebang

As Josiah rejoins them. He sees two of the Pennsylvania men, Wisnovsky and Benton, rebuilding the Pennsylvania Shebang. A few feet away Tyce looks up at him —

> TYCE
>
> Bring any grub?
> *(when Josiah indicates no,*
> *but Gleason over there is. . .)*
> Know why I joined this army? I'm not like one of your farm boys. Days I didn't work, I didn't eat. Figured at least get three meals a day . . .

He snorts at the irony. Josiah sympathizes but doesn't know what to say to him, so goes a few feet away to where the still-bloody and now-subdued McSpadden, and the now—and evermore—shirtless Billy, again despondent, are sitting in the ruins of what was Dick Potter's Shebang. He hunkers down next to them, concerned about McSpadden.

JOSIAH
How's the shoulder? How's the eye?

WE NOTE: Something new in Josiah's demeanor. Whether it's Mc-
Spadden's condition, or Dick's death, or the realization of where
they are and what it will take to survive—he has fewer illusions and
more determination, and authority, than he did two days ago.
And something has gone out of McSpadden, and Josiah is aware of
that, too.

JOSIAH
Go find some clean water, Billy, so we can clean the
Sergeant up. Trade for it if you have to.

BILLY
Yes, sir.

Josiah waits for Billy to go and then says very quietly and privately, for
McSpadden alone—

JOSIAH
Know how many they've got lying in the Dead House,
just from today? Forty-six. . . .

MCSPADDEN
God in heaven.

JOSIAH
Two by the Raiders—one shot at the Deadline—the
rest starved or . . . I dunno. They look water-bloated.
(then—)
They've tied names on tags around the big toes of
most of them. I guess so when they bury 'em there'll
be some kind of record.

MCSPADDEN
(a moment before—)
You do that for Dick?

JOSIAH
(yes; then —)
He was telling me about the water here. Can't drink
from the Swamp. Kill you . . . Have to tell the boys.

McSPADDEN
Tuck! Thomas! Wisconsin!

Their POV of Tucker, Sweet, Blackburn

Tucker looks over, comes to join them. But—

—(Thomas) Sweet and his new best friend, Martin Blackburn, pay no
attention to Josiah but instead look at—

Their POV of Munn, Collins

—and two hundred other Raiders in front of their comparatively fine-
looking tents. Munn is plucking away slowly and badly on the BANJO
while the other Raiders are eating and, considering the circumstances,
eating grandly: Curtis is gnawing on a chicken bone, someone else is
sopping up vegetable leavings from his tin plate with a large hunk of
bread, another Raider eats an apple and—

Close on Collins

Lord of the Manor, in his green coat, on his chair—his throne, really—
being shaved and barbered by one flunky while another greases his
boots.

Munn's slow banjoing displeases him. He gets up, grabs the banjo from
Munn, gives it to another Raider.

COLLINS
You call that music? I've heard better noise come out
of dried chicken guts! Give us something a man can
dance to!

The Other Raider

The other Raider hits a fast chord, smiles ingratiatingly at Collins. This one knows what he's doing with a banjo.

WIDER of The Raiders starting to sing, to clap hands, to dance.

One of them invites Collins: Lead us in the dance. . . .

Collins

Collins needs no encouragement. He starts to dance a jig. He becomes the center of attention of all his sycophants who clap hands rhythmically for him and cheer him on.

Sweet, Blackburn

Just the two of them, looking at the Raiders.

> SWEET
> Is that your banjo, Martin?

> BLACKBURN
> Was.

Sweet looks at the Raiders with an unblinking eye.

Their POV of the Raiders

Munn, in the safety of his crowd, waves, mocking them.

Some of the other Raiders start to dance around Collins as . . .

Full Shot Our Group

Tucker, 2nd Wisconsin, Billy and Tyce have gathered around Josiah and McSpadden. Gleason and Tobias and Benton, from the Pennsylvania group, are nearby. To Josiah—

[77]

2ND WISCONSIN
How's your Sergeant?

TYCE
He don't look so good. Took a crack in the eye.

MCSPADDEN
I can see we're none of us no better looking than we
were yesterday.

A growl. The men look at him and are worried. But Josiah, taking
charge, says . . .

JOSIAH
Tuck—we need some shelter here. You'll have to sew
us up something. . . .

TUCKER
Got my kit last night. My needles, thread, shears—

From the sidelines, Benton helps out.

BENTON
Somebody'll have some. Got some buttons? Brass
buttons? Everybody wants them. (They) trade 'em to
the Rebs for stuff.

JOSIAH
(nods; to Tucker)
We'll get you needle and thread. Everyone who still
has gum blankets or shelter-halfs give 'em to Tuck.
He'll cut 'em up, make us a Shebang. We'll stay right
here—

TUCKER
(If) it was good enough for Dick (it's good enough
for me). . . .

JOSIAH

I need two dollars for a Guard, to send a letter to
Dick's father.

None of the Massachusetts men has any money. Seeing this, Martin
Blackburn, the Pennsylvanian, leaves Sweet and comes over, takes off
his shoe, gives Josiah two greenbacks. Everyone is grateful.

JOSIAH

Last night, 'fore it happened, Dick was telling me
about the water here . . .
            (again calling . . .)
Thomas. Over here.

Med. Shot on Sweet

But Sweet is still ignoring him, still looking at the dancing Raiders.
Martin Blackburn rejoins him.

Gleason and Tobias come back with the bag of meal and the sticks of
wood. THEY SEE AND HEAR as—

SWEET

We'll get it back.

Sweet takes a step toward the Raiders. Gleason intercepts him, grab-
bing his arm—

GLEASON

Don't be a fool. There's ten of them for every one of
us—and besides—

Sweet shakes him off, starts walking toward the Lions' Den. Gleason
is angry.

Close on Josiah

Seeing. He stands.

> JOSIAH
>
> Thomas!

Moving with Sweet

Thomas ignores Josiah, keeps going toward the Raiders.

Gleason, Blackburn

When Sweet doesn't stop, his new friend Blackburn shrugs apologetically to Gleason and follows Sweet. Gleason, angry, stops where he is—for now.

Josiah, Our Group

Looking after Sweet. Josiah, too, is angry at Sweet's foolhardiness, but in answer to Tucker—

> TUCKER
>
> What's he doing??

> JOSIAH
>
> Whatever—
> *(stands)*
> —we can't let him do it alone.

Led by Josiah, they head toward the Raiders and finally even Gleason, who sees all this as foolishness incarnate, comes along.

Close on McSpadden

He tries but cannot make it off the ground. He watches from his knees and then tries again, this time makes it, and starts after them.

The Raiders

Waiting, seeing them coming. They slow, then stop their dancing.

Close on Collins

Alertly slowing his dancing, watching Sweet, ready for trouble.

Full Shot

Sweet and Blackburn get to the Raiders ahead of the rest of Our Group. To Munn and the Raider with the banjo—

> SWEET
> That belongs to him (Martin). We want it back.

> COLLINS
> You do, do you? . . .
> *(then, taunting—)*
> Who's your best man?

Full Shot

The rest of Our Group arrives, looks at each other. Josiah finally speaks for all of them. Meaning Sweet . . .

> JOSIAH
> He is.

> COLLINS
> That's the best you've got? He's a ba-by!

> MUNN
> Runt of the litter. . . .

The Raiders laugh, mocking Sweet.

Josiah knows better. The look he exchanges with Tucker promises a surprise for the Raiders.

Draw the ring, boys.

(calling)

Hey! Georgie!

As some of the Raiders happily draw a circle, GEORGIE, the biggest, roughest man anybody ever saw, gets easily off the ground, taking off his shirt as he does. As big as Sweet is, Georgie has height, weight and years on him.

Around them the cry goes up—'Fight! Fight!'—'Georgie and a Babee!'—and the Raiders crowd in, while—

Full High Shot to Other Parts of the Stockade

Some, not all, of the other Prisoners come from other quarters. There are two reasons why everyone doesn't hurry to crowd in: These are the Raiders and to be avoided, and fights are not unusual in Andersonville.

One who does come—We Note—is Limber Jim, the tall and rangy Woodsman, strong, fearless, incorruptible.

Curtis

The co-leader of the Raiders, Curtis, holds up a hand against the approaching prisoners.

CURTIS

Stop, right there.

The Approaching Prisoners

They do stop—which creates a No Man's Zone from which they can watch the fight, but from a distance. . .

. . . And shows the easy authority of Curtis over all of them . . .

. . . except Limber Jim, who keeps coming, pushing forward and pointing at Josiah and Sweet . . .

> LIMBER JIM
> I'm with them . . .

Curtis

Seeing it's only one, he lets him in as . . .

Collins

. . . calls cheerfully . . .

> COLLINS
> Any wants to come in for a good look, come ahead—
> five dollars a man—

. . . and laughs at them . . .

The Stopped Prisoners

grumble silently but don't move—all except little Patrick, The Drummer Boy, who slides on through.

Back to Scene

Sweet is unbuttoning his own shirt in answer to Georgie's stripping for action. Martin Blackburn is worried for Sweet and warns him privately—

> BLACKBURN
> Look out for him, Thomas. He's a bad 'un. He's killed
> men in fights in here.

Collins (played by Frederick Coffin), the leader of the Raiders, gives encouragement to Georgie, portrayed by Gary Lee Davis (left), before his fight with Thomas Sweet.

LIMBER JIM
(arriving)
Whatever you do, don't turn your back on him.

PATRICK

He don't fight fair.

But Sweet pulls his shirt over his head and is in this most vulnerable of positions when—

WE SEE COLLINS nod tautly to Georgie—

—and in response Georgie walks in without warning and slugs Sweet in the stomach, knocking him down.

Our Group, led by Josiah, is shocked and protests. So do Limber Jim and little Patrick.

The Raiders—Curtis as well as Munn and Collins—cheer and laugh.

Georgie struts around and poses like a happy victor.

> COLLINS
> We should get you three of 'em next time, Georgie—
> make it a fair fight.

Mad Matthew cheers and jumps.

And one Confederate Guard in a tower nudges another and points and laughs, too.

Sweet gets up onto his hands and knees and clears his head. He gets up.

McSpadden makes it to the outskirts of the watching crowd, forces his way in closer.

The Fight begins.

At first it goes badly against Sweet—Georgie is both brutal and dirty—and Sweet absorbs terrible punishment—

—to the dismay of his friends—

—the amusement of the Guards in the Tower—

—and the glee of the Raiders—

—but slowly the tide turns and Sweet starts giving Georgie a beating, fair but devastating—

—to the delight of Josiah and McSpadden and their friends, including Limber Jim and Patrick, who are the ones making the noise now—

—and the concern of the increasingly-subdued Raiders—

—except for Curtis, who gives another taut nod, this time to Munn, who can't stand what he's seeing—

—and, with Sweet near final triumph, with Georgie hanging on glassy-eyed and certain to go down for the count—

—Munn grabs a heavy wooden club and waits until Sweet's back is turned and then brains him. Sweet goes down—

—as Our Group, now including Limber Jim, howls in rage and tries to get at Georgie, at Munn, at everyone—

—but they are half a dozen among hundreds of Raiders, who surround them and act on Collins' command to—

COLLINS

Hold 'em! Hold 'em!

—while other Raiders turn, away from the ring—

—toward the other prisoners, the spectators—

—and, with weapons and menace, keep them frozen in place—

—across the No Man's Land—

At the Ring

Collins sees Sweet struggling helplessly to get up and kicks him—

Our Group

Josiah, Martin Blackburn, Limber Jim—even McSpadden—struggling furiously, protesting, but unable to break loose.

LIMBER JIM

You dirty coward—!

At the Ring

This time it's Munn who kicks Sweet and he is about to do it again when—

Josiah

—breaks through and gets into the ring.

> JOSIAH
> That's enough!

Full Shot

And Josiah, alone with Sweet, surrounded by weapons-bearing Raiders, would be next, except—

> LIMBER JIM
> He said that's enough, Collins!

Collins

—holds up his hand and, with humor, surprisingly agrees.

> COLLINS
> What the hell—We've had our fun for today, boys.
> You want to leave something for tomorrow, don'tcha?

And with the toe of his boot, he gets under Sweet's shoulder and flips him over, onto his back. And says to Limber Jim—

> COLLINS
> Next time, Limber Jim, it'll be you and me—

Limber Jim doesn't back down.

Full Shot

And—it's over.

The Raiders pull back, let Josiah and Martin Blackburn and Limber Jim and the others pick up Sweet and carry him off, past Collins and the other laughing Raiders—

—while the Prisoners watching across No Man's Land melt away.

Following Our Group

All the way back to the Shebang.

When they get there, Josiah tries to thank Limber Jim, but he short-cuts that.

LIMBER JIM
You're the ones went down there.

And he walks back where he came from. Josiah looks after him: That's a man to remember.

SWEET
We didn't get it back, did we?
(no)
I'm sorry, Martin.

BLACKBURN
Next time.

GLEASON
(angrily)
There'll be no next time. There'll be no more fighting, no more worrying about Raiders, no wasting time, no wasting strength—no anything. Do you want to get out of here! Do you want to live!
(shoving a canteen-half at Sweet)
Then tunnel!

BENTON
Give him time, John. Have a (heart)—

GLEASON
You too!

[88]

Sweet spits out a tooth, chastened, takes the half-canteen and crawls inside the Shebang. Benton takes the other half, follows Sweet.

Dissolve To:

Int.   Inside the Pennsylvania Shebang — Day

One of the Pennsylvania miners, Wisnovsky, lifts himself out of the hole, spitting dirt and gasping for air. He gives his bags of dirt to Gleason and Martin Blackburn and goes outside—

—passing Josiah, who is sitting alone near inside the entrance of the Shebang with his pencil and paper, frustrated, angry, not writing.

Billy comes up out of the hole with his bags of dirt.

> GLEASON
> No more for you. You've been down three times today—

> BILLY
> Not so hot down there—
>
> No Rebs—
>
> Quicker we get it dug—

Down he goes again. Gleason shrugs to Martin Blackburn.

From where Josiah sits near the entrance to the Shebang, out of his frustration—

> JOSIAH
> What do I write Dick's father? . . . "wasn't the Rebs killed him, sir . . . our own boys here did it" . . . ?

Neither Gleason nor Martin has an answer for him. Josiah puts the paper aside.

JOSIAH

How many Raiders are there?

GLEASON

Two-three-four-five hundred.

BLACKBURN

More keep going over to 'em every day—get hungry—scared—

JOSIAH

Way I see it, they're the enemy now—three years it's been the Rebels—now on in here, it's the Raiders, just as much—what they did to Dick—we can't let that happen to any of our men ever again—else we're not fit to wear the uniform—that's the way I see it.

Martin does not disagree with him—but Gleason . . . !

GLEASON

Now listen, Corporal—get hold of yourself—lot of good men have died in here—more than you know—lot more going to—

But I'm getting my men out of here, through this hole in the ground—

So we're not going back over there to kill Raiders or do anything else—

We're tunneling, understand! You want to do something useful like getting together with some others, keeping a watch—that's fine. But that's all—understand me!

Josiah understands him.

Ext.   Outside the Pennsylvania Shebang — Night

The night of the fight with Georgie . . . The night of the day when Sweet and the others have been ordered to do their hard tunneling by

Gleason. Under the stars, Thomas is bruised and dirty. He looks to Martin Blackburn, his new friend. . . .

SWEET

Martin . . . ? It doesn't scare you, being down under the ground . . . ?

BLACKBURN
(not really)
It's what I do—what I've always done—since I was eight years old—

SWEET

Was it hard the first time?

BLACKBURN

My father took me . . . I wanted to go . . . all his friends worked in the mine . . . Sergeant Gleason's father . . . Tobias' . . . I couldn't wait. . . .

SWEET

How'd you learn to play banjo?

BLACKBURN

Father taught me that, too. . . .

SWEET

Really think I can learn?

BLACKBURN

I could tell the other night. Could tell right away . . . You'll be good . . . real good. . . .

Blackburn smiles at him. Thomas smiles back. HOLD.

Fade Out.

Fade In:

Ext.   Inside the Stockade — Day

Josiah, Martin and Tobias squatting in intense conference with a dozen other prisoners near the Swamp.

Here are Limber Jim, their fierce ally from the fight with the Raiders, and Samson, the one-legged man with crutches, the firebrand, an ally—

— and WILLENS, a Sergeant, cautious, a mediator.

And the silent and wretched GRUNDY, who sits on the edge of the crowd and listens but says nothing.

> WILLENS
> We'll stand watch with you.

> SAMSON
> Long overdue, I say.

> LIMBER JIM
> Why just a watch! Why not wade into 'em—knock their heads off! That's what we ought to be talking about!

> WILLENS
> Keep your voice down—!
> *(then—)*
> You can't just wade into 'em. There's too many of 'em.

> SAMSON
> We'll get every man here—Should'a done it two months ago—
> - (MORE) -

SAMSON (cont.)
(disgusted)
—just that everyone thought we was gonna get exchanged—Sure we will—any year now—

Did it when we should'a, my brother'd still be alive.

TOBIAS
Josiah . . . ? Maybe we should take 'em on . . .

LIMBER JIM
What are we feared of! We're not little girls, y'know!

But Josiah makes no comment. He wants to hear more.

WILLENS
You can't keep a secret in a place like this—you start
to put a thousand men together to take 'em on—
'cause that's what you'd need—they'll get you first.
They will. And there's a reason I don't want to do anything just now. Some of us are working on a tunnel
out of here—

TOBIAS
Well so are we but—
(to Josiah)
—what do you think?

Martin Blackburn gives Tobias a swift, sharp look, says nothing.

Josiah looks at all the men waiting for him to speak.

JOSIAH
For now we'll all keep watch—not go after 'em—but
any the Raiders come for—the others'll help out.
We'll all stand up for each other.

Nobody say yes if you don't mean it.

All the men agree.

Limber Jim and Samson are disappointed but accept it.

And on the edge of the circle the wretched Grundy still sits and says nothing.

Moving with Josiah, Martin Blackburn, Tobias

Walking back to their Shebang.

> JOSIAH
> You shouldn't have said that, Toby, about us working on a tunnel—

> TOBIAS
> I know—soon as I said it—

> BLACKBURN
> There's Tunnel Traitors here turn you in for half an apple—

> TOBIAS
> *(lamely)*
> I just thought—they were making all these excuses—

> JOSIAH
> We'll have to tell John.

Tobias knows. It doesn't make him feel any better.

Inside the Shebang — Day

OPEN CLOSE on Gleason. Very angry.

> GLEASON
> We'll all work double shifts now—everyone of us—
> tunnel has to be rushed now—whether we're hungry
> - (MORE) -

Left to right, McSpadden (Frederic Forrest), Billy (Jayce Bartok), Wisnovsky
(Olek Krupa), at their Shebang.

> GLEASON (cont.)
> or tired, doesn't matter—we don't have a month any
> more—

> TOBIAS
> I'm sorry, John. I know I—

> GLEASON
> And you three—
> *(Josiah, Tobias, Martin Blackburn)*
> —get outside—watch everyone who heard you—any
> of 'em's a Tunnel Traitor, goes near a Reb—

You know what to do. Josiah and Martin Blackburn nod, go outside.

Before Tobias follows, he looks at Gleason, chastened, apologetic.
Gleason turns away from him, angry, to the only other man in the tent,
Tyce, who waves his disgust at Tobias.

[95]

GLEASON
(to Tyce)
Get some plates. We're going down.

The hole, over there . . . the one Billy is coming out of, again, pushing more dirt ahead of him.

Gleason waits for him to clear the hole and he and Tyce start down.

Ext.   Full Panning Shot Of The Stockade — Day

FROM HIGH ANGLE CAMERA SLOWLY PANS THE ENTIRE STOCKADE. . . .

WE SEE:

The men . . . the lassitude . . . sick call . . . the Towers . . . the ball-and-chain . . . the Raiders . . . guards . . . the Swamp . . . some movement here and there . . . bathing and washing at the Swamp . . . men walking around . . . and watching all this:

Near the Shebang

Josiah . . . Martin Blackburn . . . Tobias . . . standing a few feet apart from each other, watching different parts of the camp . . . concentrating hard, not looking at each other.

As usual, Martin Blackburn is more serious and wiser, Tobias more impulsive and less understanding as . . .

BLACKBURN
Josie? . . . All those letters home . . . How do you send 'em?

JOSIAH

I don't. No money.

TOBIAS

What's the point of writing 'em, then?

Who'd want to hear about this stinkhole anyway?

You write about Devil Wirz and the Raiders?

Josiah's shrug indicates—Sometimes.

Martin senses, almost subliminally, a reticence, a shyness in Josie—
which he respects, but which also makes him curious.

BLACKBURN

What else, Josie? . . . I got a letter out to my wife and
children when I first got here, telling 'em I was all
right . . . I was thinking about them . . . what do you
write about?

JOSIAH

My friends . . . some things I think about . . .
                    (like what?)
Oh—
          (he is shy about personal things)
—how it's hard to understand how a place can be as
bad as this—and how there's good here, too.

TOBIAS

Good?? Here? The only good in here is getting out of
here and the sooner the better.

Patrick, the Drummer Boy, comes happily by. . . .

PATRICK

Hear what happened?
                    (no . . .)
                - (MORE) -

[97]

PATRICK (cont.)
One of the Minnesota boys—fainted dead away—
they thought he was gone for sure—took him to the
Dead House, laid him all out, toe tag and all—an
hour later—whoops—he sits up quick—

—and this Reb pup jumps six feet straight up in the
air—about comes out of his own scared-y skin—
                    (mimics, stuttering . . .)
'Hey there Yank—if you ain't dead, you get back
inside!'

Josiah and Martin—not Tobias—reward Patrick with smiles and a
laugh, and off he goes, laughing delightedly.

Josiah and Martin Blackburn's eyes haven't stopped sweeping the com-
pound. Continuing as before . . .

BLACKBURN
Josie? Like what? . . . What's good in here?

JOSIAH
Friends who'll help you, no matter what . . . who'll
be your friend—like you and Thomas are friends—
no matter what.

A little embarrassed . . . a little awkward . . .

They continue to scan the camp slowly, carefully. For a long time,
INTERCUTTING them and what they SEE, nothing . . .

And then Josiah SEES . . .

Long Shot   Josiah's POV of Grundy

The wretched Grundy, trying not to look conspicuous and therefore
very conspicuous, as he furtively walks in an indirect path toward a
Turkey Roost which holds Lt. Barrett.

Resume Josiah, Martin Blackburn, Tobias

Josiah watches long enough to be sure and then says . . .

JOSIAH

There.

Martin and Tobias look at him. Where?

There.

Tobias goes quickly to the Pennsylvania Shebang.

Inside the Pennsylvania Shebang

—Where Gleason is at the mouth of the tunnel, receiving a couple of platefuls of dirt from Tyce. Tobias enters and, urgently—

TOBIAS

John! John!

Gleason quickly follows him out to—

Outside the Shebang

—where Martin Blackburn points out Grundy moving furtively toward Lt. Barrett's Turkey Roost, looking around him, trying to be sure he's unobserved. Gleason waits just a moment to be sure. Then—

GLEASON

Quickly. Quickly now.

Follow me. And off they all go.

Josiah

Alone, pushing through people, moving down the hill fast, never taking his eyes off Grundy—

Gleason, Martin Blackburn, Tobias

Gleason leading the others downhill fast, stripping off his coat, pushing through people as he comes, saying to everyone as he forces his way through—

> GLEASON
> Be ready, be ready . . . look lively, look lively . . . Be
> ready. . . .

The word is quickly passed. Everyone is instantly ready, everyone is focused—for what they do not all know. But they get up off the ground—Limber Jim and little Patrick do—and look after Gleason, and they follow along as—

Resume Grundy

Approaching Lt. Barrett, who is alone in the Turkey Roost. Grundy stops at the Deadline, turns, checking to make sure he isn't being observed.

Moving Shots — Josiah, Gleason

Coming after him.

They are taking different routes down the hill—Josiah still alone, Gleason leading the others, including Martin Blackburn and Tobias—trying to move quickly without seeming to.

Grundy, Lt. Barrett

Grundy, at the Deadline rail, not daring to call, whispers loudly . . .

> GRUNDY
> Lieutenant . . . lieutenant . . .

Lt. Barrett does not hear him.

Moving with Josiah, Tobias, Martin Blackburn

As they quicken their separate paces down the hill. Little Patrick is with them, moving fast. . . .

Grundy at the Deadline

Takes another look around. He doesn't see the drama building quietly behind him, he still thinks he's safe—so, a little louder—

> GRUNDY
> Lieutenant . . . Hey, lieutenant . . .
> *(getting his attention)*
> Got something for you.

> LT. BARRETT
> What'cha got for me, Yank?

> GRUNDY
> I'll meet you at the gate. Right now, all right?

> LT. BARRETT
> Tell me what you got.

> GRUNDY
> I can't . . . Not here . . .
> *(looks around)*
> I got informa . . .

At which time Josiah arrives at the Deadline, ten yards or so away from Grundy, and he calls up to Lt. Barrett . . .

> JOSIAH
> I got a letter to be mailed, sir. Can you help me with
> it? I'm told it takes two greenbacks . . . ?

He holds the letter and greenbacks up toward Barrett.

> LT. BARRETT
> Is the letter unsealed? I'm gonna read it.

> JOSIAH
> Yes, sir, it is.

> LT. BARRETT
> Meet me at the gate.
> *(to Grundy)*
> You too. . . .

Barrett swings his look back to Grundy at the exact moment that—

Gleason

—and Martin Blackburn and Tobias get to Grundy. Gleason slams his coat down over the startled Grundy's head and grabs him by the head as Tobias and Martin get him by the feet and they instantly hustle him back away from the Deadline into the massed crowd of alerted prisoners who make room for them and then close like the Red Sea, swallowing them—

Lt. Barrett in the Turkey Roost

Unholstering his pistol, surprised and angry. Where's Grundy?!

> LT. BARRETT
> Hey! Hey now!

Barrett's POV into the Prisoners

As they close ranks, swallowing Gleason and the others. At first they look innocent and then one or two brave souls, led by Patrick (teasing) and Limber Jim (mocking him)—

PATRICK

What'cha looking for Lieutenant? . . . Lose something, did you?. . . .

LIMBER JIM

I'll tell you what he's looking for—a thirty-day furlough, Reb son-of-a-bitch.

Josiah

Melts back into the crowd, his work done.

Lt. Barrett (and Other Guards)

Peering into the mass below, not seeing anything, furious but helpless.

LT. BARRETT

Where is he now?! You give him over, you Yankee sons of bitches!

Patrick, Limber Jim, the Others

Laughing at him, not giving an inch.

Gleason, Tobias, Martin Blackburn

In the middle of the sheltering mass, flat on the ground, holding the struggling Grundy still, Gleason tightening the coat around his head. HOLD and then—

Fade Out.

Fade In:

Ext.   The Moon Over Andersonville — Night

The barest sliver of a moon in a partly cloudy sky. Thousands of men in the open field . . .

. . . and dozens of Guards in the towers.

Inside the Pennsylvania Shebang — Night

Our Group all jammed in tight: Josiah with McSpadden on one side of him and shirtless Billy on the other, Tucker, 2nd Wisconsin, Tyce, 60th Ohio, huge Sweet and little Blackburn sitting together, best friends . . . and all the other Pennsylvania men: Wisnovsky, Tobias and, nearest the entrance, Benton. Only Gleason, their Leader, is missing.

A few weeks have passed. They're all dirtier than before—they've been digging in the earth.

They wait in silence until, up from the hole in the ground, Gleason struggles and appears, spitting dirt.

They all look anxiously at him until he gives his verdict—

> GLEASON
> Good tunnel. It'll hold.

All the Pennsylvania men are relieved, even self-congratulatory. They sit back pleased. Especially Tobias—

> TOBIAS
> Considering the little time and the tools we had—

> GLEASON
> *(cutting him off)*
> It's good enough for what we need.
> *(then—)*
> All right—first men out have the best chance—more time before they sound the alarm—

WISNOVSKY

More time to get away from their damned hounds.

GLEASON

—so we'll draw lots to fix the order we go in.

JOSIAH

No—we've talked it over—
                    (we Massachusetts men)
—you go first. It's your tunnel.

GLEASON

You helped us dig it.
                    (to the filthy Billy)
You—you're a tunneling fool—you ever get to Pennsylvania, I'll have work for you.

BILLY

Never going underground again. Going back to New Bedford. Breathe good salt air.

JOSIAH

Fair's fair. You first.

GLEASON

All right. Agreed . . . We need one strong man to be last—brace the beam—make sure everyone gets through before the support gives 'way—we have a cave-in, he's got to drag us out fast.

SWEET

I'll do that.

GLEASON
(no)
Has to be a mining man. Someone who can see a cave-in coming.

BLACKBURN
I'll stay with him.

Cementing their already close friendship. Gleason: agreed.

WISNOVSKY
What do we do with him?

Him—Grundy, whom we now SEE for the first time, tied and gagged in the corner.

60TH OHIO
Leave him tied up there for another week. Be good for him.

WISNOVSKY
Kill him.

TYCE
Cut his scummy throat for him.

Wisnovsky pulls out a jackknife, opens the blade. Tyce grabs Grundy by the hair, yanks his head back to expose his throat to Wisnovsky. Grundy struggles. Muffled protests of terror.

McSPADDEN
(no)
He's not going anywhere. I'll keep watch on him. I'm staying anyway.
(to Josiah)
I'm not fit to go. Really I'm not. . . .

This is news to the Massachusetts men. They all look shocked and protest. Josiah stays calm.

JOSIAH
All we have to do is get to the river.
(to Gleason)
What's that, a mile or two?

GLEASON

Can't tell from the map.

JOSIAH

Leave him tied. Someone'll find him in the morning.
                    (to McSpadden)
You're coming with us.
                    (to Gleason)
How soon do we go?

McSpadden shrugs, goes along passively but gratefully.

GLEASON

Looked to me like we only have a few more feet to
dig. We can break through in an hour.

WISNOVSKY

We should go first chance, John. Those hyena Raiders
over there, they may come after us anytime—

TYCE
(kicking Grundy)
—or sell us to the Rebs for a crust of moldy bread.

He grabs the feet of the trussed and helpless Grundy, wrestles the good
boots off Grundy's feet. Now Tyce takes off his own torn and almost
worthless boots—the sole flaps loosely on one of them—and puts on
the new ones. He jams his old boots in his belt and sits back, pleased.

Tobias looks at his own bare feet, looks at Tyce.

Tyce sees and ignores him.

Everyone is aware of the looks. No one likes what Tyce is doing—not
doing—but no one interferes.

Wisnovsky has been thinking. He looks from Grundy to Josiah. . . .

WISNOVSKY

Have to kill him. Can't leave him to turn Traitor on
someone else's Tunnel.

GLEASON
(after thinking it over)
He's right, Josie—

WISNOVSKY
(takes out his knife again)
Should'a killed him soon's we caught him—

TYCE
(angry)
Do it. I'll do it. I want to get out of here, out of here,
out of here!

Josiah holds up his hand. Don't do it. And there's a stalemate until—

GLEASON
(to Wisnovsky)
Give me the knife.

JOSIAH
(a quiet warning)
John—

GLEASON
I'm not going to kill him.

He goes quickly to Grundy, who is screaming and thrashing in muffled
terror (and then pain) and, blocking our view of Grundy, does something. Then he steps back and we SEE the blood-red TT Gleason has
cut on Grundy's forehead. Grundy has passed out in shock.

GLEASON
Boys'll all know he's a Tunnel Traitor now.
(then, to Benton)
How's the moon?

Benton quickly lets himself out.

Josiah and McSpadden and the others accept Gleason's justice. In the
Silence—

[108]

ANDERSONVILLE PRISON

AS SEEN BY

JOHN L. RANSOM,

AUTHOR AND PUBLISHER OF "ANDERSONVILLE DIARY, ESCAPE AND LIST OF THE DEAD,"

Head Quarters,
Rebel Camp,
Hospital,
Cook House,
Death House,
Death Line,
the Island,
Sutler's Camp,
Police Quarters.

10. Hospitals along the Dead
11. Market Street,
12. Broad Street,
13. Inside Stockade,
14. Second Line Stockade,
15. Third Line Stockade,
16. Lieut. Head Quarters,
17. Washing Place,
18. Rifle Pits,
19. Astor House Mess

A drawing of Andersonville by John L. Ransom, prison survivor and diarist. This is the stockade at its fullest, in the summer of 1864, when 33,000 Union soldiers were imprisoned there. (Courtesy Andersonville National Historic Site)

New prisoners, known as "Fresh Fish," being marched from the train past the guard encampment indicated by the number 12 in the lower right-hand corner of the drawing. (Courtesy Andersonville National Historic Site)

A soldier in tattered uniform scoops up his daily ration of cornmeal. In the background, other prisoners are herded into the stockade. The drawing, dated 1896, is by J. E. Taylor. (Courtesy Andersonville National Historic Site)

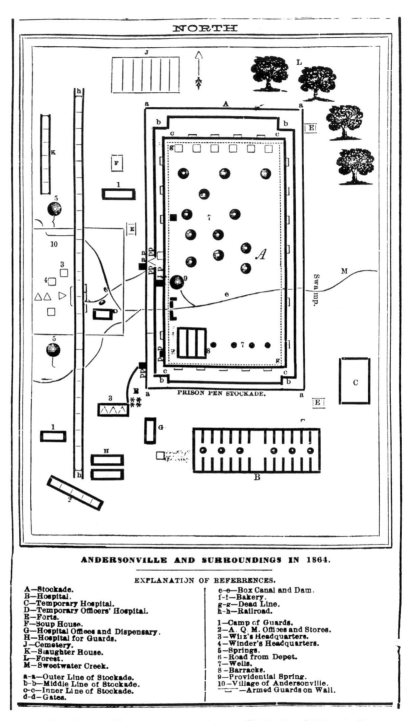

A map of Andersonville. (Courtesy Andersonville National Historic Site)

Half the stockade is visible in the foreground of this period drawing, while a train can be seen in the background. Note the sluggish stream, also known as "The Swamp," which was the only water supply for the camp. (Courtesy Andersonville National Historic Site)

The Shebangs, in a photo taken from a Turkey Roost. The Deadline is visible on the right. (Courtesy Andersonville National Historic Site)

Men crowded into the stockade. (Courtesy Andersonville National Historic Site)

The latrines, shown at the foreground of this photograph, were known as the "Sinks" and were located at the edge of the Swamp. (Courtesy Andersonville National Historic Site)

A soldier's drawing of his fellow detainees at their Shebang. (Courtesy Andersonville National Historic Site)

Father Peter Whelan, the much-loved Georgia priest and Confederate chaplain who comforted many prisoners. Whelan escorted the six Raiders to their execution. (Courtesy Andersonville National Historic Site)

The execution of the Raiders' six ringleaders, in a drawing made by a fellow prisoner. Collins, at the extreme right on the gallows, falls as the rope breaks. Historically, he was hauled back up and rehanged. (Courtesy Andersonville National Historic Site)

A burial party placing bodies in one of the mass graves at Andersonville.
(Courtesy Andersonville National Historic Site)

Camp Commandant Captain Henry Wirz, the only man executed for war crimes after the war, at his hanging on November 10, 1865, in the courtyard of the Old Capitol Prison in Washington, D.C. (Courtesy Andersonville National Historic Site)

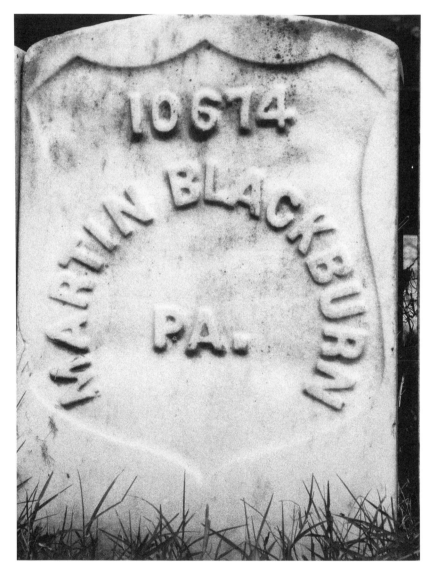

The headstone on Martin Blackburn's grave at Andersonville. (Courtesy Andersonville National Historic Site)

The Massachusetts Memorial at Andersonville. (Courtesy Andersonville National Historic Site)

The present-day field at Andersonville.

BLACKBURN
We get any thinner, we can escape out a worm hole
'sted of a tunnel.

Ext.   Benton Outside the Pennsylvania Shebang — Night

Benton looks up at the sliver of moon in the cloudy sky, then ducks
back inside.

Inside the Shebang — Night

Benton returning.

BENTON
A sliver, and it's cloudy besides.

Gleason nods and pulls out the hand-drawn map, starts to pass it
around.

GLEASON
Nobody can take this—if you're caught it'd lead 'em
to the rest of us—so study it 'til you know the way.

As the men study and pass the map, Gleason is looking hard at Tyce.
Tyce sees and tries to ignore him but Gleason is unrelenting. Finally—

GLEASON
Give him your old boots.

Gleason snaps a look at the barefoot Tobias: Yes, him.

Tyce is defensive, stubborn, angry—and alone. He sees everyone looking at him. To Tobias, finally, and unbending—

TYCE
You got anything to swap?

No. Tobias doesn't. Stalemate. Looks all around.

Gleason slices the three precious brass buttons off his coat, gives them
to Tyce, and with cold force says—

GLEASON

Now do it.

Tyce shrugs, looks at the buttons appreciatively—pretty good deal—pockets them, hands his old boots over to Tobias. As Tobias puts them on—

—Josiah passes the map to the next man.

JOSIAH

Let's make 'em divide their forces. You go right out-side, John, we'll go left. . . .

GLEASON
(nods—agreed)

One more thing. We won't all get away. Whoever does is honorbound to get to Grant or Sherman—tell 'em what it's like in here—how many of their men are dy-ing—and they've *got* to exchange for us.
(then, to all—)

We'll go in two hours. With God's luck, we'll meet at the river.

He reaches over and shakes hands first with Josiah and then with McSpadden.

Ext.   **Outside the Pennsylvania Shebang — Night**

. . . where Billy speaks privately to Josiah.

BILLY

You need help with the Sergeant?

JOSIAH

No—I'll be with him—I want you to be the first Mas-sachusetts man out—you run for the river—

BILLY

I'm going to get there, too.

JOSIAH

Yes you are.

Patrick Shay, the cheerful drummer boy, appears. Happily . . .

PATRICK

Hey, Josie . . . hey, Billy . . . Hear what happened—?

JOSIAH

Tell.

PATRICK

One of the guards had this pet dog he really favored, see, only he got loose and run inside the Stockade. Some of the Illinois boys catched him and you can just imagine how long it took to pop that ol' doggie into their stew kettle—so an hour later when the Reb comes by and says real sad-like 'Any you boys seen my little doggie?,' know what they said to him?
(no—what?)
Didn't say nothing'! Just rubbed their bellies and went Roof!, Roof!, Roof!

He rubs his belly and laughs. Billy is too tense to laugh. Then Patrick turns serious—

PATRICK

Good luck tonight.

BILLY
(astonished)

You know?

JOSIAH

There's not much in here Patrick doesn't know.
(to Patrick)
- (MORE) -

The Confederate guard at Andersonville.

> JOSIAH (cont.)
> May be room for one more. I could ask Sergeant
> Gleason.

> PATRICK
> Nah—thanks anyway, Josie—some of the boys here
> sorta depend on me—I think I'd better stay.

> Hope you make it.

And off he goes. They watch him disappear. HOLD.

Ext.   Outside the Stockade Walls — Night

SHOOTING FROM A LOW ANGLE up to the walls and the guard
towers. The guards are lounging easily, looking into the Stockade, away
from CAMERA.

It is amazing how much light even a sliver of moon casts.

The ground outside the prison is cleared for a long way—as much as 200 yards—in every direction, giving no hiding place to an escaping prisoner.

In the FOREGROUND, the earth moves and then WE SEE Gleason's head appear. He lifts himself out of the hole, quickly looks up at the towers from his crouch, then reaches a hand down the hole. He pulls up Wisnovsky. As quickly and quietly as they can, off they go, into the woods on the right.

The guards do not turn around.

Tobias comes out, pulls Benton up. They check the towers and then take off for the nearby woods on the right. . . .

Now Billy and then Tucker . . . then Tyce alone . . . then 2nd Wisconsin and 60th Ohio follow them out. They all go to the left.

Miraculously, the Guards do not hear, do not turn.

Josiah helps McSpadden out. They look up at the towers and start off fast, duck walking. They have gone left, and are half way to the tree line when—

—a tree root trips McSpadden and he goes sprawling. He and Josiah immediately freeze on the bare ground.

Med. Shot   Tower from their POV — Night

—but a Guard thinks he's heard something. He turns around quickly and looks at the area. He nudges his companion and they both look.

Ext.   Outside the Walls — Night

Close on Josiah, McSpadden. Frozen on the ground, not daring to move.

Tower Outside the Walls — Night

The Guards are still looking, still alert, 'though less so. . . .

Resume Close on Josiah, McSpadden on the Ground

. . . and Josiah and McSpadden are getting ready to make their move, only not quite yet . . .

Tunnel Exit Foreground, Guard Tower Background

. . . when Martin Blackburn wriggles out of the hole. Miraculously the guards don't see him.

He waits, crouching, by the hole—

Close on Josiah, McSpadden

—as Josiah and McSpadden SEE and hold their breath—

Tunnel Exit

—and then Sweet's head appears. He reaches up a hand and Blackburn helps pull him out of the ground. It's a struggle, little Blackburn and big Sweet, but finally Sweet is out—but it's noisy, and a tremendous exertion—

Up Angle to Tower

—and the Guard hears and sees.

> GUARD
> Hey!

He quickly aims and SHOOTS.

Other Towers

Other Guards in their towers SEE and SHOOT. The cry goes up . . .

> GUARDS
> Yankees escaping! . . . Outside the walls . . . ! East
> Wall, East Wall!

Resume At the Tunnel Exit

Sweet and Blackburn, unwounded so far, make a run for it.

Josiah, McSpadden

They, too, jump up and run for the tree line.

Tower

A Guard takes a bead on Sweet, shoots.

Sweet and Blackburn, Running

Sweet falls, shot in the back.

> SWEET
> Martin . . . !

Blackburn, a few feet ahead of Sweet, turns around and stops.

Josiah and McSpadden at the Tree Line

They get to the trees, and temporary safety. They stop and turn—

> JOSIAH/McSPADDEN
> Run, Martin! Run!

Close on Sweet

And Sweet tells Blackburn the same.

> SWEET
> Run, Martin. . . .

Close on Blackburn

But Blackburn does not run. He walks back and stays with Sweet, cradling his head.

> BLACKBURN
> I'm here, Thomas. . . .

Josiah, McSpadden at the Tree Line

Josiah and McSpadden know they can do nothing more for Sweet or Blackburn. They exchange an anguished look and take off, running through the woods, bullets spattering around them. McSpadden does not run well and Josiah has to encourage him and, at times, wait for him.

Towers

. . . as the Guards shoot and reload.

Ext.   Kennel Outside the Walls — Night

The hounds are baying and jumping in excitement. Their handlers come in quickly, open the doors, get ready for the chase.

Full Shot on Lt. Barrett, A Dozen Soldiers

Running for all they're worth, dressing and loading as they come. As they pass the kennel on the way to the horse corral, the dreaded Lt. Barrett in the lead—

LT. BARRETT

    Let 'em go!

A handler lets the dogs out and they start to sniff the ground and race around as Barrett and his men continue to the corral at full speed.

Tracking with Josiah, McSpadden Through the Woods — Night

Running for all they're worth. McSpadden still has trouble keeping up with Josiah, who waits for him, urges him on.

Corral Outside the Walls — Night

Out come half a dozen guards on horseback, flying, Lt. Barrett in the lead. They pass . . .

. . . a group of guards on foot, running after the prisoners . . .

. . . and race off with the dogs, splitting and going in two directions. . . .

Resume Josiah, McSpadden

Running through the woods and—

—into a swamp, HEARING THE FARAWAY BAYING AND SHOUTING. McSpadden stops for a moment to LISTEN.

McSPADDEN

    Dogs!

God, I hate dogs. It spurs them on.

Blackburn and Sweet at the Tunnel Exit

Blackburn is still cradling Sweet when . . .

. . . Barrett and his horsemen and the dogs charge into view. Barrett sees Blackburn and Sweet and . . .

> LT. BARRETT
>
> There's some!

The dogs and men race for them. The dogs start to savage Sweet and the helpless, terrified Blackburn. A guard runs up, jabs Sweet with a bayonet as someone else restrains the dogs, calls up to Lt. Barrett about Sweet . . .

> GUARD
>
> This one's dead.

> LT. BARRETT
> *(seeing the dogs take off)*
>
> There's more!
> *(a quick look at Martin)*
>
> Take that one back!

As two Guards yank Martin to his feet, march him back toward the out-buildings . . .

. . . Lt. Barrett whirls his horse and leads his men in pursuit of the dogs, who are on Josiah and McSpadden's trail. . . .

Series of Shots of Josiah and McSpadden and their Pursuers

Struggling through the Swamp.

McSpadden is breathing hard and he slows . . .

. . . and then HEARS something and stops. Hissing . . .

> McSPADDEN
>
> Listen—!!

WHAT HE AND JOSIAH HEAR: One pack of the hounds has caught up with and is tearing into one or some of their fellow escapees. It is an AWFUL SOUND, faraway but full of man's anguish and desperation and the dogs' blind and unstoppable mission. When the LAST CRIES CEASE . . .

. . . McSpadden and Josiah resume running, McSpadden staggering forward through the muck and vines. . . .

Resume Intercutting

The dogs, after them, stopping to get the scent, then tearing off again—

And Barrett and his men charging ahead—

Josiah, McSpadden at the Edge of the Swamp

Running until McSpadden can run no more. He stops, gasping . . .

> McSPADDEN
> How far's . . . the river . . . ?

Josiah looks around, SEES a little hillock. Leaving McSpadden, he runs up the little hill and—

Josiah's POV of the River

—he can see The River!, not a quarter of a mile away.

Josiah

> JOSIAH
> I can see it!

He runs back down the hill to McSpadden at the edge of the swamp, to give him strength and courage, but McSpadden is too far gone.

> McSPADDEN
> Can't make it . . . Go on . . . without me . . . Go, Josie. . . .

But Josie bends, lifts McSpadden onto his back, carries him up the hillock. They plunge downhill toward The River in the distance, staggering on across the field.

We Continue Intercutting . . .

Barrett and his horsemen, struggling through the swamp . . .

And the baying hounds flying through the dense woods. . . .

Josiah and McSpadden in the Field

Staggering on, toward the river. There is, ahead of them in the field, one and only one tree.

Over the Hillock into the Field

—here come the hounds, into the field.

Josiah and McSpadden in the Field

Josiah with McSpadden still on his back. As weak as he is, he still runs as hard as he can, as long as he can. And then, finally, the hounds are almost on them. . . .

> McSPADDEN
> Those dogs, Josie—!

I don't want them getting into me. Josiah, knowing his fear, SEEING and HEARING the closing dogs, knows they have no chance and no choice.

Josiah alters course and heads for the tree. They get there and Josiah climbs or jumps up onto the first tier of branches and, using all his strength, pulls McSpadden up—

The Dogs in the Field

—and they are barely up in the tree before the hounds arrive and jump around the tree, crazed—

Med. Close on Josiah, McSpadden

Josiah is behind McSpadden, his arms around him, hugging him close to prevent him from falling from their precarious low perch. He is trying to reassure McSpadden—I've got you, Sergeant—but his face shows all the despair in the world.

McSpadden is afraid and is kicking out to keep the jumping dogs away.

Wider Shot on Lt. Barrett and his Troop

Barrett charges over the hillock and toward them on horseback. He takes his pistol out as he comes.

When he gets to the tree, he is enraged and looks as if he will shoot them—but finally doesn't.

Full Shot

Of Josiah and McSpadden up the tree, the hounds baying and jumping, and Barrett's angry soldiers circling on horseback below . . .

. . . and a short distance away The River. HOLD in the moonlight.

Fade Out.

Fade In:

Ext. Outside the Star Fort — Day

We HEAR RAGGED MUSIC from the Star Fort in the distance, the Fife-and-Drum playing of an unpolished military band . . .

. . . as WE SEE Colonel Chandler and his aide, Lt. Dahlgren, the Confederacy's Inspectors, heading from the Stockade toward the Star Fort. Colonel Chandler looks unhappily at . . .

. . . Our Group in the Stocks, the medieval devices of torture outside the Stockade: here, spread-eagled in what looks like a mass crucifixion, are Josiah, McSpadden, Billy, Tyce, Tucker, Martin Blackburn, Wisnovsky, Tobias, Benton, 2nd Wisconsin and 60th Ohio.

Ext. Inside the Star Fort — Day

A very young Fife-and-Drum Corps composed of both Confederate soldiers and Prisoners, none older than sixteen, playing raggedly—

—as the Soldiers in the Star Fort march in formation to the music, not much more competently—

—and Wirz is furious. To Lt. Barrett—

> WIRZ
> These "musicians"—they must be much, much better! And this what-you-call-marching! You will drill them until it is dark, and after dark if necessary! They must be ready tomorrow!

> LT. BARRETT
> Absolutely, Captain. They will be.

The Band, the Soldiers, have heard it all. So have—

—Colonel Chandler and Lt. Dahlgren, who now come into the Star Fort. Chandler looks at Wirz and the Band and drilling soldiers, all with contempt. Misreading the signs—

WIRZ

So, Colonel—I hope you do not have to leave before
we have the chance to welcome back General
Winder—

CHANDLER

I'm leaving tomorrow morning—

WIRZ

Too bad—they will improve very much bef—

CHANDLER

If you spent one hour a day improving the conditions
of the Stockade instead of planning these ridiculous
little ceremonies—

He gestures, then turns and walks away with Dahlgren. Wirz turns
pale. He rushes to catch up with Chandler—

WIRZ

Colonel—excuse me—you must know—I am responsible for the Guard Force here so their performance—

CHANDLER

You are also responsible for the operation of the
prison—

WIRZ

Well yes—in part—but Colonel—

CHANDLER

May I ask you a personal question, Captain Wirz?
Something I need to know for my report—

WIRZ

Of course. Anything—

CHANDLER

I have heard that before you came here from Switzer-
land ten years ago, you had medical training—

WIRZ
Absolutely true, Colonel—I am fully qualified to—

CHANDLER
—to allow this disgrace to civilization—?

WIRZ
Colonel, please—you must not say these things in
front of my men—

CHANDLER
They'll hear soon enough. I'm filing my report as
soon as—

WIRZ
There are things I must say to you—but not in front
of the men—I must talk to you—please—

Chandler, finally, barely, reluctantly relents and lets the desperately
anxious Wirz steer him and Dahlgren into his quarters—

Int.   Wirz's Quarters in the Star Fort — Day

—Where a window is open, so part of the confrontation will be heard
anyway by—

Ext.   Outside Wirz's Quarters — Day

—The Soldiers still at attention and by the youthful Band, which is
rehearsing all the way through—

Int.   Wirz's Quarters — Day

WIRZ
You must know, Colonel—General Winder, he is in
charge here—totally—of food, medicine, supplies—

CHANDLER

I know what the General's responsibility is. If you
want to discuss your own responsibility for the deaths
of more than one hundred men in your care a day—

WIRZ

Of course—I only meant—

CHANDLER

You, Captain—in one week you could have finished
dams across the streams—made floodgates to flush
out the waste! You could have built another camp to
relieve crowding—

WIRZ

Yes, but you see we have no tools—I asked for saws
and axes, not once but ten times—

CHANDLER

You have some tools, Captain. I have taken inventory.
You could have paroled prisoners to bring in food
from nearby plantations—

WIRZ

I did, Colonel—earlier—they ran away—

CHANDLER

—under guard!—and let the prisoners build shel-
ters—

WIRZ

We had no canvas—

CHANDLER
(the woods)

Wood!

WIRZ

—I wanted them to have wood but General Winder—
he ordered all the trees cut down so there'd be no
shade—

CHANDLER
I said I won't speak to you about General Winder. If
you have anything to say on your own behalf—

Wirz looks defeated. A moment. Chandler, seeing Wirz has nothing
more to say, starts to exit with Dahlgren. Then—

WIRZ
I—most respectfully—
(searching)
—please—you must tell them—there is no one, absolutely no one in this war who has to deal with the
circumstances I have to deal with. I do not complain.
I am a soldier, Colonel—I know my duty and I do it
faithfully—look at this arm of mine, shattered in the
Battle of Seven Pines—

CHANDLER
Yes you are a soldier, Captain—

—so when you personally ordered stocks to be built,
and the ball-and-chain—

WIRZ
—only for escaped prisoners—so they won't run—

CHANDLER
—you knew you were violating The Articles of War.
As you were violating them when you withheld food
as punishment.
(a long moment before—)
Was there anything else you want to say, Captain?

It is over. Wirz is devastated. Or is he—? He walks away, and then
makes . . . his difficult confession . . .

WIRZ
It is true, Colonel. Of course it is. It is all true.

I know it will not surprise you that I agree with what
you say. I try—I try very hard—those young boys in
- (MORE) -

[126]

the Fife-and-Drum Corps out there—I paroled them so they would not have to stay in that wretched Stockade—I did that—I ordered the hospital moved outside the walls where the air is better—I ordered the Stockade made bigger—

—but they just send us all the time more prisoners—on General Winder's orders—33,000 now when we were built for only 8,000—

—so of course I agree with you—with proper help, we could do much more. The problem is, I need people. Can you help us there, Colonel? . . . You know, if I were Major, instead of only Captain, then I would have more staff assigned to me. We could start to solve these problems, together.

They listen to you in Richmond, Colonel. I think if you put that recommendation in your report, it would be most definitely helpful.

Chandler looks from Wirz to Dahlgren. He is speechless. HOLD.

Ext.   Full Shot in Front of the Stockade — Night

The moonlight shows us:

Our Group imprisoned in the stocks. Josiah, McSpadden, Tucker, Martin Blackburn and Wisnovsky, Billy, Tyce and 2nd Wisconsin, Tobias and Benton and 60th Ohio—all are there. Several of them are not standing but have collapsed, and are kept up only by the devices and not by their legs.

A flatbed cart is near the stocks.

A few sentries on duty.

WE SEE Colonel Chandler and Lt. Dahlgren approach on the road. They stand near the stocks. Then, from his deepening depression—

                          CHANDLER
There will be those who know we tell the truth and
will want to act on it. But—men have other things on
their minds these days and I fear nothing will be
done. . . .

Good night, Lieutenant.

                        LT. DAHLGREN
Good night, sir.

Leaving Chandler, Dahlgren walks past the stocks. HOLD Chandler
foreground until Dahlgren calls. . . .

                        LT. DAHLGREN
Colonel—couple of these here are dead—least two of
them—legs gave out and they strangled themselves.

More hard news. Then—

                          CHANDLER
You think Captain Wirz knows?

                        LT. DAHLGREN
I don't know if he does, sir.

                          CHANDLER
Go tell him.

                        LT. DAHLGREN
Yes, sir.

Not that Chandler expects it to make any difference. Dahlgren goes
to—

Ext.   Captain Wirz's Quarters — Night

An outbuilding with two SENTRIES in front.

In LONG SHOT WE SEE Lt. Dahlgren arrive and speak to a SENTRY,
who then knocks on the door.

A long moment and then Wirz appears in his nightclothes. Wirz and Dahlgren have a discussion, STILL IN LONG SHOT, and then Wirz speaks to the Sentries. They salute and Wirz goes back inside the house as—

—the Sentries and Dahlgren go to the stocks and let the men out, to collapse onto the ground.

Closer Shot At the Stocks

It is hard to know who is alive and who isn't, so little is the difference between Life and Death in the men on the ground.

The Sentry bends over and checks the men.

>   SENTRY
> These here are still alive, I think . . . Them two are
> gone.
>   *(straightens up)*
> Lieutenant, you mind helping me get these here ones
> back inside the walls?
>   *(to Sentry #2)*
> Eugene, get them two to the Dead House.

It is still not clear who is dead and who is alive, as Sentry #1 rolls the flatbed cart over. He and Dahlgren load the survivors onto the cart, and—

—WE SEE Josiah and McSpadden, Billy, Martin Blackburn and Wisnovsky, 2nd Wisconsin and Tyce, Tobias and Benton all put on the cart, groaning in misery and barely conscious.

The Sentry and Dahlgren wheel the loaded cart back to the Stockade.

The two bodies left on the ground, dead, staring up at the moon through sightless eyes, are Tucker and 60th Ohio.

And Colonel Chandler looks down at his shoes and contemplates man's inhumanity to man.

Fade Out.

Fade In:

Ext.   A Small Country House — Day

And Sweet is happily feeding his hogs in the pen around the side.

Something is odd here. The FILM IS SLIGHTLY FOGGED . . . THE CAMERA SLIGHTLY TILTED . . .

. . . and when Josiah comes INTO SHOT, THERE IS A BIT OF GLARE that comes with him.

> JOSIAH
> Come inside, Thomas.

> SWEET
> I will, Josie. Soon as I finish taking care of my animals.

He smiles warmly at Josiah, who moves toward the house, passing Tucker, who is sewing a shirt and who looks up and smiles at him—

> TUCKER
> Be with you in a minute, Josie.

Fine. Now Josiah looks up, outside the gate, where he SEES—

—an anxious and ragged Tyce standing, hat in hand, hoping to be asked in. Josiah waves him in cheerfully and they go together into the house.

Int.   Kitchen of the Country House — Day

Josiah walks with Tyce to the kitchen dining table and they sit, joining—

—Josiah's cousin Bob Reese, Bob's wife Sarah and their little boy. Bob is eating and also feeding the little boy as Sarah looks on with love.

At one end of the table Dick Potter and his fisherman father mend their fishing nets—

—and at the other Josiah's reserved Father looks up from his newspaper.

Tyce ignores everybody and eats greedily.

In the kitchen, Josiah's MOTHER prepares more food and brings it to . . .

. . . the table, already groaning with turkey, ham, beef, potatoes, gravy, biscuits, vegetables, cider.

Josiah's mother adds a huge scoop of mashed potatoes to Josiah's already-full plate and ladles gravy over them. Josiah, his mouth full, looks up at her and smiles back and mumbles his thanks: this is good! She puts her hand on his head and smiles and says—

JOSIAH'S MOTHER
I love to see my boys eating well. Don't you, father?

The Father looks up and also smiles as . . .

FARAWAY VOICE
Fresh fish!

Cut To:

Close on Josiah

as his eyes blink open. The Dream is over and we are back in . . .

Ext.   Inside the Stockade — Day

New Union prisoners, men who have seen their share of hard fighting, have just come in through the main gate—and in the familiar scenario, Wirz is with his guards giving his familiar speech—

Those who are not shot are caught by the dogs without fail and put in the stocks or ball-and-chain . . .
and *still*, if you escape the dogs, to go hundreds of
miles to your own army? Not possible . . .

The Raiders

DURING THE ABOVE: Munn and Collins and all the other Raiders,
200 or more, listening to Wirz from close by and looking at the new
men with light in their eyes, ready to pounce at the first oppor-
tunity. . . .

Our Group Outside the Shebang

A hundred yards away, on the slope of the hill. . . .

Josiah, now fully awake, lifts himself up, painfully, to look. We NOTE
he has more hair, more beard, both unkempt. His face has a newly-
gaunt quality.

Our Group, also looking at Wirz speak to the new prisoners, has gone
through terrible changes. Gone, of course, are Sweet and Old Dick,
Tucker and 60th Ohio. Of the Pennsylvania miners, Gleason is gone.
The survivors WE SEE HERE—Josiah, McSpadden, Billy, Martin
Blackburn, Tobias, Benton—are all in increasingly wretched shape,
showing the effects of prison life and of the escape attempt and its
aftermath, lying or sitting on the ground, unable to move without pain.
Now and from here on, they are increasingly indistinguishable from
the most ill-dressed and sun-roasted and wretched of the Old Prisoners. Hair, beard, color, clothing, in some cases posture.

There is one new member of The Group: Limber Jim, the strong and
rangy prisoner who came to their aid in the melee with the Raiders
after Sweet's fight against Georgie. He is in better shape than the rest
of the Group, whose every joint and muscle still shows the effects of
the stocks. As he feeds the near-helpless McSpadden a bit of mush with
his fingers . . .

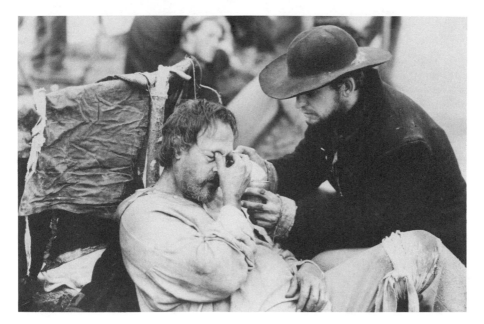

Following the failed escape attempt, Limber Jim (portrayed by Peter Murnik), at the right, tends the injuries of Sergeant James Dudley McSpadden (played by Frederic Forrest) of Company I, 19th Massachusetts Volunteers.

> LIMBER JIM
> How you feel, Sergeant?

> McSPADDEN
> Never better. . . .

Limber Jim continues to nurse and feed his helpless friends with his fingers, little bits of mush, as they are in no shape to care for themselves.

> LIMBER JIM
> Everybody's saying you got real close. Closer than anyone ever did. . . .

> McSPADDEN
> Saw the river. . . .

> LIMBER JIM
> Could Sergeant Gleason have gotten away? Really— away?

Time passes slowly as a pensive Martin Blackburn (played by Ted Marcoux) of the 184th Pennsylvania, and Josiah Day contemplate the failed escape attempt foreground, as Limber Jim, in the background, prepares to bring them their rations.

McSPADDEN

Chance.

JOSIAH

Good chance.

Billy is only a few feet away, curled up, in total despair, his back to them, staring at nothing through dull, vacant eyes. Little Patrick tries to feed him but—

BILLY

Don't want it—

McSPADDEN

Eat, Billy—you haven't eaten in a week—can't live without eating—

BILLY

Don't want to live—not here—gonna walk across
the Deadline—

McSpadden and Josiah are shocked. They look at each other before—

BILLY

Gonna die anyway.

McSpadden looks to Josiah for help. Josiah tries a different tack. . . .

JOSIAH

Going to leave the rest of us alone in here, Billy?. . . .

When Billy doesn't answer, Josiah crawls over and with his last re-
maining strength shakes Billy angrily.

JOSIAH

We're in this together. We're gonna get through this,
together—or we won't—together. Don't make it easy
for 'em.

Now eat!

For a long moment, as Josiah and McSpadden and Limber Jim wait
anxiously, Billy doesn't move. Then he finally forces himself up into a
sitting position and lets Patrick feed him.

You can almost hear Josiah exhale. McSpadden too.

Limber Jim

Stands and looks with dark anger to where Wirz has finished his
speech to the new prisoners. HE SEES—

His Long POV to Wirz, Munn, New Prisoners

—Wirz leave. Munn has arrived and is chattering away as he steers the
unsuspecting new men . . .

MUNN
Up here's the place to go—nice and dry up here—we
got some food, too—where'd you boys get catched
at?

. . . toward the hidden, waiting Raiders who now pounce on and savage the new men.

Close on Limber Jim

He watches the Raider assault until the end, his fury building. HOLD,
and then—

Dissolve To:

Ext.   The Stockade at Peace — Day

Time has passed. The Stockade is even more crowded, with only a few
feet, even inches, between men.

Josiah at the Massachusetts Shebang

He takes a stub of pencil and his paper and with stiff, awkward fingers
slowly starts to write—

JOSIAH'S VOICE OVER
It is now some weeks since we tried to get away from
here and since our time in the Stocks without food or
water. I am now able to write, and to stand for a short
time. Yesterday I even took a few steps, 'though a
comic sight it must have been.

During the Above, the Camera Drifts Off to Show . . .

. . . the Men, sun-beaten, with white cracked lips and flaming shoulders and necks, sitting all through the Prison, bored and vacant, most

doing nothing but staring at the ground or walking aimlessly . . . scratching, or cleaning their toenails, or shaking lice out of their hair and beards.

JOSIAH SEES: 2nd Wisconsin down at the Swamp on all fours, drinking greedily. He finishes and stands painfully and looks around—guiltily? defiantly? No. Nobody notices or cares.

Outside the Shebang — Day

Wisnovsky limps by. McSpadden, sitting alone, still in difficulty from the after-effects of the Stocks, raises a stiff and awkward arm to get his attention. All very privately, very quietly—

> McSPADDEN
>
> Olek—
>
> *(sit a minute . . .)*
>
> You went out the tunnel with Gleason. . . .
>
> *(yes . . .)*
>
> What happened to him?

> WISNOVSKY
>
> *(looks around before—)*
>
> The dogs—dogs got him—I got up a tree—he wouldn't come up with me—wouldn't stop—kept running for the river—swinging a stick at those dogs—you can't outrun dogs—

> McSPADDEN
>
> *(swears before . . .)*
>
> I heard 'em get someone . . . Glad I didn't see it.

> WISNOVSKY
>
> I'm not telling them (the others)—No point in it—he was like a father to 'em—I say I don't know—he could have got away—I didn't really see—

It's very, very hard news, but McSpadden nods. That's the right thing to do. . . .

Resume Josiah

Still writing slowly and with difficulty.

> JOSIAH'S VOICE OVER
> Sitting all day long, I now think I know what the real
> enemy is in here—

Now he LOOKS AT something that disturbs him. He SEES—

—A hundred feet away, Mad Matthew is trying to eat his food undisturbed but Tyce, of Our Group, is badgering him (SILENTLY FROM OUR AND JOSIAH'S POV), trying to wheedle him out of it.

Closer on Tyce, Mad Matthew

Mad Matthew tries with hurt eyes and hunched shoulder to protect his food, to turn away from Tyce, but Tyce is reaching for the food, trying to take it without making a commotion. Mad Matthew is defenseless as . . .

. . . nearby, other men watch and one may even call something critical to Tyce, who snarls at him to mind his own business.

DURING THIS, WE SEE Josiah stop writing to watch what's happening. Josiah stands—

—and the almost-broken McSpadden manages to lift up and watch as—

—Josiah leaves the Group, limps down, and from behind clamps a hand down on the startled Tyce's shoulder and (SILENTLY FROM McSPADDEN'S POV) remonstrates with him. Leave Mad Matthew alone! Sullenly, defensively, Tyce backs off . . . and Josiah tells the grateful Mad Matthew it's all right, and touches him gently on the arm, saying (SILENTLY) that he won't bother you anymore . . .

Josiah Day washing his laundry at the "Swamp."

. . . and Josiah returns limping to Our Group's Shebang where he sits next to McSpadden. He looks over the Camp and picks up his pencil and paper and says, as much to himself as to McSpadden—

> JOSIAH
> It's not the Rebs make 'em do these things—not the
> Raiders—it's having nothing to do—

> McSPADDEN
> *(didn't hear clearly—)*
> What, Josie?

> JOSIAH
> Having nothing to do all day long—that's what eats
> at 'em.

McSpadden looks around. It's true. The boredom, the isolation, the loneliness and despair are enemies, too. HOLD INTO—

Dissolve To:

Ext.   Near the Massachusetts Shebang — Day

OPEN CLOSE on Limber Jim, looking down from the Massachusetts Shebang toward the Main Gate, again in silent fury as—

At the Gate

Wirz is with his guards, giving some New Prisoners his familiar speech—

> WIRZ
> Tunnels are useless. Even if you are outside, I give any two men a full day's start and then track you with the dogs—but why bother anyway?—

—while nearby Munn and Collins and all the other Raiders listen to Wirz and look at the new men, ready to go into action as soon as Wirz leaves.

Our Group at the Shebang

Featuring Tobias and Benton. They are aware of what is happening. They LOOK AT—

Our Group's POV to Wirz

Going on as before . . .

> WIRZ
> I know for absolute fact that at this moment talks are going on for Exchange of Prisoners—any day you will
> - (MORE) -

WIRZ (cont.)
be paroled in quick order. So. We understand each
other.

Our Group   Favoring Limber Jim, Tobias, Benton

TOBIAS
(calling, croaking . . .)
You're a damn liar, Wirz!

BENTON
(maybe . . .)
If John Gleason gets to Uncle Billy or ol' Ulyss . . .
(to his friends . . .)
. . . then we'll get exchanged, you bet on it.

Limber Jim has something else in mind. With his growing anger . . .

LIMBER JIM
Look at those vultures, waitin' to rob and murder the
new boys. Look at 'em!, the dirty little cowards. . . .

Josiah, McSpadden, Martin Blackburn, the others who are lying
around struggle up off their backs to look at:

Their POV of the Raiders near Wirz

Lying in wait. The Raiders SEE Wirz finishing his speech . . .

WIRZ
So . . .

And he is off under guard, leaving the Stockade. As soon as he's
gone . . .

. . . Munn comes forward to the new men.

MUNN

Hey, Fresh fish!—welcome to Andersonville—
(his expansive wave)
—fine looking place, don'tcha think? . . . For a hog
pen maybe . . . You some of Grant's men from up in
Virginia? That where you get catched at?

As Munn continues his patter, steering the new men toward the Raiders . . .

MUNN

Let me show you around, get you a decent place to
stay. You want to be up away from the Swamp . . .

. . . as WE SEE the waiting Raiders with their hidden clubs and knives.

Series of Shots

Everybody, all the Prisoners, looking down at the lambs being delivered to the wolves—hating it, but weak, disorganized, lifeless, helpless to do anything about it.

Our Group

Favoring Limber Jim watching the Raiders. It is more than he can bear.
Very agitated . . . !

LIMBER JIM

Something! Anything!

What? What do you mean? Limber Jim starts scrabbling in the dirt
with his fingernails. . . .

LIMBER JIM

Who's got something for me to use? Anything!

He finally comes up with a rock as big as his fist. He looks at it with a
glint and starts to his feet. His friends are alarmed . . .

Oh Jim, don't! There's a thousand of 'em.

BENTON
They got knives and clubs and—!

LIMBER JIM
(on his feet)

Who's with me!

Josiah, McSpadden, Martin Blackburn don't know what to make of it. But Jim—

—is an Avenging Angel framed against the sky, the rock held aloft in his fist.

LIMBER JIM
WHOOOOO??

Breathless, Our Group looks at him.

Long POV Shot Toward the Raiders

Munn has delivered the unsuspecting new men to within inches of their doom at the hands of the Raiders—

—when both groups stop to look up at the strange, howling apparition above them.

Close on Limber Jim

As before.

LIMBER JIM
WHOOOOO?? Who's with me? WHOOOOO?

Limber Jim and Our Group

As Limber Jim starts down the hill, alone, toward the Raiders.

Our Group looks at each other in wonder and then back at Limber
Jim. . . .

There he goes. . . .

LIMBER JIM

WHOOOOO??

Our Group

McSpadden struggles to get off the ground as he mutters as much to
himself as to The Group . . .

McSPADDEN
We're with you . . . we're with him. . . .

. . . but he can't make it off the ground until Josiah pulls him up. Martin Blackburn and Wisnovsky also struggle up as . . .

Limber Jim

Still striding alone, holding his rock high—

LIMBER JIM

WHOOOOO??

Close on the Raiders and their Would-Be Victims

Looking up at Limber Jim. What the hell is this?

The new prisoners don't understand. . . .

Another Group of Prisoners

Faraway, Samson struggles up, calls . . .

SAMSON
I'm with you, Jim!

Twenty yards away another man gets to his feet.

Our Group

Although it is hard for them to stand, they struggle up and, with Josiah
and McSpadden, take faltering steps forward as . . .

McSpadden

    With you, Jim!

Moving with Limber Jim

Advancing toward the Raiders. He thrusts his rock into the air and . . .

Limber Jim

    WHOOOOO??

Other Prisoners

Rising, one here, one there, three here, a dozen there . . . and starting
down the slopes toward the Raiders.

The Raiders

Munn and Collins, especially, have the sense to be very alarmed.

Collins

    Form up! Form up!

Moving with Limber Jim

As he is joined by a few men, lame, crippled, weak, and strong men,
too. Their ranks start to swell—

Moving with Josiah, McSpadden, Martin Blackburn

As they struggle to catch up, limping, being passed by other men in
better shape. . . .

Many Shots

. . . of Prisoners from all parts of camp in ones and twos and eventually hundreds, giving VOICE and joining the surge down the hill.

Samson, the one-legged man, comes swinging hard down the hill on crutches FOREGROUND, passing others like the wind, determined to be in on this.

Even Patrick, the Drummer Boy, is racing along.

Only Mad Matthew stands and watches, his fingers in his mouth, not understanding what's happening.

Moving with Limber Jim

. . . in the middle of an Army as they now break into a FULL-THROATED ROARING RUN down the hill. . . .

Moving Shots

Limping gamely ahead, Tobias, Benton, 2nd Wisconsin, even Tyce and Billy. . . .

The Raiders, the New Prisoners

Astonished by this Avalanche thundering down on them from all sides . . .

. . . the new men as well as the Raiders.

The Raiders try desperately to form themselves into a tight defensive circle, Georgie at the point, eyes wild and bright, ready for the onslaught, animals at bay.

Most have grabbed—do now grab—whatever they can use for weapons: clubs, knives, blackjacks, a shovel, pointed stakes, rocks, anything. Munn worms his way backwards and hides in the middle.

Many Shots

As Limber Jim's army smashes into the Raiders—as Limber Jim smashes into Georgie, bowling him over—and the rest of his Army roars in with him and overwhelms the Raiders, annihilates them, swallows them.

The new Prisoners look on bewildered and untouched.

Samson flails away with one of his crutches, a maddened, hopping stork, catching and almost decapitating Munn.

Limber Jim has the sleek Collins by the throat, down on the ground, and is trying to choke the life out of him.

Around them, the fight is going on, overwhelmingly one-sided.

Curtis

One of the Raiders' leaders, the maddened Curtis, breaks out of the pack and, swinging a spade and bellowing, races out into the camp.

Men—scarecrows—fall back from his screaming charge.

He is heading on a collision course for—

Josiah and McSpadden

Josiah does not fall back. He gets in front of McSpadden and stands his ground as Curtis, spade held high, rushes him, swinging, trying to crush Josiah's head.

Josiah catches the spade, holds it, forces, forces it back until finally Curtis is down and Josiah holds him on the ground, the spade handle across Curtis' throat . . .

. . . and McSpadden rips his own shirt into strips and starts to tie Curtis up. . . .

Series of Shots

Of Limber Jim and his Army destroying the Raiders with fists and the Raiders' own weapons until . . .

. . . all resistance is ended . . .

. . . and Josiah and McSpadden and some others push the bound Curtis ahead of them, back into the pack of defeated Raiders . . .

. . . and Mad Matthew arrives to jump up and down excitedly at the scene, happy but uncomprehending . . .

. . . until finally a MIGHTY TRIUMPHANT ROAR goes up from every quarter, shaking the prison. HOLD this great triumph, both for those who fought it and those who, too weak to fight, cheered it on. . . .

Fade Out.

Fade In:

Ext.   The Raiders' Treasure Trove — Night

It is Night and a fire is burning down Collins' wooden hut in the background, while foreground—

—WE SEE a vast treasure trove in a large pit in the ground. Uniforms, haversacks, utensils, weapons, watches, books, food—even Martin Blackburn's banjo—all the stolen goods the Raiders have amassed.

PULL BACK TO SHOW THAT around the pit, looking into it, ragged Prisoners stand, full of emotion. CAMERA MOVES FROM FACE TO FACE—

> TOBIAS
>
> That's Martin's banjo . . .

> AN OLD PRISONER
>
> My greatcoat. I know from the tear in the sleeve . . .

> PATRICK
>
> Wait 'til everyone's here before anyone takes anything. . . .

Another Angle (or Moving Camera)

—to where a hundred Raiders, most scared, some surly, sit jammed together on the ground, their hands tied, the shadows from the flames on their faces. They are guarded by fifty of the victors armed with the clubs and pocket knives and rocks they have captured. Georgie is in this group of Prisoners, Tyce an angry guard. . . .

And Another Angle (or Moving Camera)

. . . TO THE FRONT OF THESE where the Six Leaders of the Raiders—Munn and Collins and Curtis and the three others—all bruised, all scarred, are not just tied by the hands but are trussed, bucked and gagged, each watched individually by an angry former VICTIM standing over him as around them all (THIS CAN BE ONE CONTINUOUS SHOT) . . .

. . . while raging in front of them Limber Jim has a length of rope or cord he is snapping, testing its strength, as—

> LIMBER JIM
> *(calling over)*
>
> Hang 'em! Hang 'em all!

... as Munn looks terrified, babbling indecipherably through his gag ...

... but Collins doesn't flinch, even when they kick him. ...

> SAMSON
> String 'em up, the murderin' devils ... !

> LIMBER JIM
> *(the rope!)*
> I'm doing it with my own two hands!

McSpadden, standing with Josiah and Martin Blackburn, puts a hand on Limber Jim's arm, staying him—

> McSPADDEN
> Jim, Jim—we're not murderers—

> LIMBER JIM
> Murder?? To hang *them*??

> SAMSON
> What *they* did was murder!

> McSPADDEN
> We're not hangmen—

> LIMBER JIM
> *(to all)*
> Any wants to help, come ahead! ... Nobody has the
> sand for it, I'll do it myself ...
> *(kicking Collins)*
> ... starting with you.

> McSPADDEN
> Hold on a minute here, Jim—

JOSIAH
(a moment before . . .)
What about them?
(the other Raiders . . . not the Ringleaders)
Do we hang them too?

Josiah is standing with his Sergeant—and their questions have slowed but not stopped the demands for vengeance. But—!

LIMBER JIM
It's not murder, it's justice!

But others seem not so sure now, and then . . .

. . . Martin Blackburn patiently holds his hand up. The others see him and finally quiet down and turn to him. . . .

BLACKBURN
The first thing we must do—before anything else—is give them a trial. A fair trial, with witnesses. . . .

There are still, and again, protests: Fair trial? When were they ever fair to us, the murderin' dogs! . . . What do you need witnesses for! Everyone's seen with their own eyes!. . . .

SAMSON
Show 'em the fairness they showed my brother . . . !

LIMBER JIM
(overlapping . . .)
They killed a hundred men in here . . . !

Other Prisoners join in: 'They deserve killing! . . . It's only justice we want!'

BLACKBURN
We must put them on trial. A fair trial, with a jury. . . .

[151]

Favoring Josiah

Seeing that Blackburn is virtually alone. He waits until the uproar dies down and then says—

> JOSIAH
> Say why, Martin. Say why you think they ought to
> have a trial.

> BLACKBURN
> Are we so much better, if we do to them as they did
> to us?

The temperature is starting to change. Some of the others agree—not all, not Limber Jim and Samson, the most hot-headed—but some of the men at least stop to think. In the uncertainty that follows . . .

> JOSIAH
> That would take time. What do we do with them
> meantimes? If we keep them here—
> *(looking at Limber Jim and Samson)*
> —someone will surely kill them.

It's true, and they all know it. Some would do it personally and several Prisoners, led by Limber Jim and Samson, say so: I will! Nobody knows the answer until—

> BLACKBURN
> We'll ask Wirz to keep them under guard outside the
> walls and deliver them back to us for trial when
> we're ready.

A strange idea, and an intriguing one. The Prisoners look at each other. Should we? You think he will? Finally . . .

> McSPADDEN
> Josie . . . ? What do you say?

Everyone—it seems everyone is looking at Josiah, waiting for his decision, both sides equally.

Josiah is aware of the stakes. And he nods:

> JOSIAH
> Let Captain Wirz see how we conduct ourselves with
> men at our mercy.

And finally everyone . . . including finally even Limber Jim and Samson, both very reluctantly . . . agrees.

Int. Wirz's Office — Day

Wirz . . . and several lesser officers, including Lt. Barrett, are studying . . .

. . . the Prisoners who face them: Martin Blackburn is the Leader of the Delegation and he is accompanied by Josiah, McSpadden, three or four others. They have made their case and wait as . . .

. . . Wirz thinks hard about it. Then—

> WIRZ
> How would this trial be conducted?

> BLACKBURN
> According to the rule of law, Captain. Both sides
> would have lawyers to speak for them—Raiders
> would be allowed to speak for themselves, question
> the witnesses—

> WIRZ
> You would have a jury?

> BLACKBURN
> Yes, sir. New men who come in after today so they
> won't be prejudiced against the defendants.

WIRZ

I have never in my life heard of anything like this.
                    (to Lt. Barrett)
These men, these "Raiders"—they're as bad as they
say?

LT. BARRETT

Animals, Captain. Cutthroats and murderers. Even as
Yankees go, these are the worst of the worst.

WIRZ

If I allow this—it will make your task easier, keeping
order in the Stockade?

LT. BARRETT

Might do that, sir. They're the worst of the trouble-
makers—

Wirz walks around, thinks, looks at all the Prisoners. He seems to recognize Josiah—maybe.

WIRZ

I've seen you before, haven't I?

JOSIAH

I was one of the men caught escaping.
                    (directly, without anger)
You had me in the stocks for a week.

WIRZ

Ah! You won't make that mistake again, eh?
                    (walks, thinks, decides. . . .)
I will get you law books. Keep the proceedings in
writing. You will send the findings and sentences to
me and if everything is in order, the sentence will be
ordered for execution.
                    (to Lt. Barrett)
Keep the ringleaders under lock and key until they ask
for them.
                    - (MORE) -

[154]

WIRZ (cont.)
(to Martin Blackburn)

Go.

Have your trial.

Martin Blackburn, Josiah, McSpadden, the others, all a little surprised
he agreed.

JOSIAH/MARTIN BLACKBURN/McSPADDEN
Thank you, Captain.

As they leave, under guard . . .

Cut To:

Ext.   Andersonville Stockade — Day

A LONG, FULL PANNING SHOT as a strange, unnatural silence
hangs over the camp. Thousands of men, all standing, forming the
sides of a bowl, looking down at—

The Main Gate

Where hundreds more wait in parallel lines leading from the gate
to a . . .

Courtroom

An impromptu courtroom rigged in a hollow at the bottom of the bowl
of watching Prisoners.

MUSIC: A little trap, or snare, drum. Military, rhythmic, tense, growing, building OVER . . .

Closer Shots in the Courtroom

A jury of New Prisoners, not seen before, in comparatively clean uniforms. All are Sergeants.

The Prosecutor, HORACE TRIMBLE, a country lawyer, homespun, getting ready.

The Defense Counsel, JARED HOPKINS, New York City, sharp and competent despite his current circumstances and shabby clothes.

Josiah, McSpadden, Martin Blackburn, the rest of Our Group, near the front of the Courtroom. Like everyone else they are silent, tense, expectant, as they look at—

—all the Raiders excepting only the Six Ringleaders, including some like Georgie we have seen before. They are sitting on the ground in the front of the Courtroom with men like Limber Jim and Samson standing over them.

In the watchful, waiting SILENCE . . .

> VOICE
> *Here they come*!

Trap Drum Music Out, Sharply

And everyone, looks at—

The Main Gate

As it swings open and, with Lt. Barrett on horseback at the head and Confederate Guards aside and behind, the Six Ringleaders are brought into camp and—

—delivered to a guard of Old Prisoners who will take them the rest of the way to the Courtroom.

Now the Old Prisoners in the parallel lines come alive. They SHOUT praise for both Lt. Barrett and Wirz . . .

> OLD PRISONERS
> Good for you, Lieutenant . . . Bully for Wirz! . . . Man of his word! . . . Hurrah for the Captain!

And scorn for the Six . . .

> OLD PRISONERS
> Now we got ya! . . . How you feeling today, boys? . . . Not so chipper, eh? . . . Don't look so big today, do they? . . . Collars a little tight, are they, boys? Get a lot tighter 'fore we're through with you. . . .

Of the Six, Munn looks afraid—terrified. Collins, still an enormous presence in his green coat, is cool, contemptuous even.

And, as the SNARE DRUM comes in again, keeping the cadence, The Six are marched, under hold, all the way to—

The Courtroom

Where they are told to sit near their lawyer, Jared Hopkins. And the catcalls stop and a HUSH comes over the camp.

MUSIC: Drums OUT, sharply.

THE FOREMAN of the Jury, a tough old three-striper, stands:

> FOREMAN
> Who's speaking first?

Horace Trimble, the Prosecutor, the courtly country lawyer, stands. . . .

> TRIMBLE
> I am, Your Honor. Sergeant Horace Trimble, 9th Indiana Volunteers, appearing for the Prosecution. And may I introduce to this Court the Honorable Jared

Hopkins, Esq., 102nd New York Volunteers, appearing for the Defense. . . .

A ROAR of anger and rage and catcalling comes cascading down from the sides of the bowl.

A Stenographer waits with his pencil as . . .

Jared Hopkins, aggressive and capable, tries to speak, to be heard above the mob, but he doesn't have a chance. Every time he tries to say something the Old Prisoners on the hill howl him down with catcalls and booing—Shyster! Liar! Save your breath!

Josiah and McSpadden and Martin Blackburn exchange silent looks. They do not share this mob mentality as—

—Hopkins keeps trying but, having no chance to be heard, finally waves his hand angrily, in disgust, and sits down.

Most of the Raiders are terrified. Munn, certainly. Not Collins.

IN A TURKEY ROOST, Lt. Barrett looks down.

Horace Trimble stands, holds up his hand for quiet, finally gets it. Calling, to all—

> TRIMBLE
> It is my job to prove to these men—
> *(the jurors)*
> —who arrived here but yesterday—that the men here
> on trial behaved like savages—barbarians—and
> worse in this camp—while the rest of you are soldiers
> in the Federal Army!, who conducted and *will con-*
> *duct* yourselves accordingly.

Two faraway VOICES call: 'And sailors!' . . . 'And marines!'

> TRIMBLE
> I cannot imagine these insults and this display of tem-
> per—however justified—will help you achieve the
> - (MORE) -

[158]

The stenographer at the trial of the Raiders. Captain Wirz provided law books for reference during the trial and required that a record of the proceedings be kept.

TRIMBLE (cont.)
results we all desire. I hope we have no more such outbursts.

Mister Hopkins. I beg your pardon. Please say what you have to say, sir.

Josiah, McSpadden, Martin Blackburn look at each other. They are impressed by Trimble.

And so it seems are most of the Old Prisoners, who—after one or two more catcalls—quiet down.

Jared Hopkins stands, tautly nods his thanks to Trimble. To the jury—

> HOPKINS
> I do not envy you men at all.
>
> Yesterday you arrived in Hell.
>
> I wish for your sakes you had not. I wish you had had
> the honor, instead, the luck, the foresight, the privi-
> lege—to die in honorable battle against the Secession-
> ists. I do not speak lightly. Ask any man here—these
> unfortunates in the dock before you or those shouting
> insults down on us—
>
> —Andersonville Prison is not just a place without
> food a man can eat or water he can drink or a place
> he can come in out of the rain from—it's not just a
> place where guards murder us for their sport—it is a
> place without civilization. It is *a place without law*!

At this—Hopkins' "It is a place without law!"—Josiah frowns. He thinks about that seriously as Hopkins continues over the enraged protests from the other Prisoners—

> HOPKINS
> Andersonville *is* Hell, and you will hear how men—
> good Union men, good Federal soldiers, and sailors—
> were driven mad—

The Old Prisoners on the hill rain more scorn and anger down on Hopkins: 'They never were soldiers! . . . Never were any good! . . . Bounty Jumpers! Cutthroats! Murderers! . . .'

HOPKINS
(riding over . . .)
I will not be silenced!—were *driven* by these circumstances not of their own making to commit, *under-
standably*, acts of desperation they never would other-
wise have committed!—

LIMBER JIM
(from the hills)
We stood it!

HOPKINS
(in a fury—)
—and *I will be heard*!

Old Prisoners, also in a fury: 'We stood it! . . . Liar! . . . Shyster! . . .
String him up too! . . .'

Josiah tries to hold up his hand for quiet, gets nowhere.

Horace Trimble, too, waves to the hills for quiet. Hopkins continues
to the jury—

HOPKINS
That is the second reason I do not envy you. You are
being asked to sit in judgment on soldiers in your own
Federal Army, soldiers who are themselves victims of
Ander . . .

SAMSON
We stood it!

HOPKINS
(riding over)
. . . victims of Andersonville, whose conduct must be
understood as being *caused* by . . .

HOWLS OF RAGE pour down on him from the hills.

[161]

Josiah and McSpadden do not howl. They struggle to listen as Hopkins tries to make himself heard—

HOPKINS
. . . caused by the Rebels! They are the ones ought to be on trial before you!, not the men of your own Army.

He is finished. He could not be heard over the NOISE in any case. He sits down, waving his disgust.

The Foreman of the Jury stands. To Trimble—

FOREMAN
Call your witnesses.

Horace Trimble nods. He walks away, first to the non-Ringleaders, the Raiders including Georgie who are sitting on the ground, and says . . .

TRIMBLE
We charge these men here with being thieves who stole from their fellows food, clothing, possessions of every kind, always brutally and without mercy and frequently under cover of night.
                    (to the jury)
You will have all the witnesses to that you want.
                    (to the hills)
Is there any man here who can say they did more? Who saw one of these—

—I exempt the Six Ringleaders—

—who saw one of these commit or order another to commit murder? If so and he will swear to it, let him now come forward.

He looks into the hills, and around . . .

Full Panning Shot of the Prisoners on the Hills

Men look at each other but no one comes forth.

Med. Close on Josiah, McSpadden, Others

They too look around but do not move.

Back on Trimble

The answer he expected. He nods and walks away from—

—the suddenly-relieved Raiders at his feet—

—to the Six Ringleaders, including the still-terrified Munn and the bold Collins—

—and stands above them.

> TRIMBLE
> Is there any man here who saw one of these Six commit murder or order another to commit murder of another Federal soldier, to steal his goods or for any other reason? If so and he will swear to it, let him come forward now.

Med. Shot on Josiah, McSpadden, Martin Blackburn

Josiah comes forward. Unlike others, there is no triumph in his action; he is a soldier performing his duty.

Full Shot of the Stockade

As men, hundreds of men, start down from the hills to the Courtroom. Many have raised fists, or voices. CAMERA PICKS UP Limber Jim . . . Samson . . . some of the others.

In the Courtroom

Trimble, waiting patiently. He knows what is about to happen.

The Six, aware of the inevitable, looking around—some, like Collins, defiantly, and some, like Munn and Curtis, in fear.

Hopkins, too, sees the hundreds of witnesses coming down the hill and knows grimly and without doubt what it means.

Full Shot

As THE CAMERA PULLS BACK AND UP, WE SEE hundreds of men coming forward to testify.

Dissolve To:

Long Shot to a Witness Box

. . . or what passes for a Witness Box, near the Jury. Limber Jim is answering Trimble's questions. . . .

Dissolve To:

Different Long Shots Toward Witness Box   Later in the Day

. . . as first Willens and then Samson and, as we DISSOLVE AGAIN, an unknown Old Prisoner or two, all answering Trimble's questions and speaking to the Jury, and then . . .

Sergeant Horace Trimble (Tom August) of the 9th Indiana Volunteers, the prosecutor in the trial of the Raiders, questions a witness. The judge is portrayed by Dale Fetzer, a Civil War Re-Enactor and Military Consultant to the picture.

Dissolve To:

Close   Shot on Josiah — Still Later

Josiah gives the oath with his hand on the Bible and waits for Trimble to say—

TRIMBLE
Tell the jury what you have seen, Corporal.

JOSIAH
Yes, sir. I—ah—before I do—
(to the Foreman)
- (MORE) -

[165]

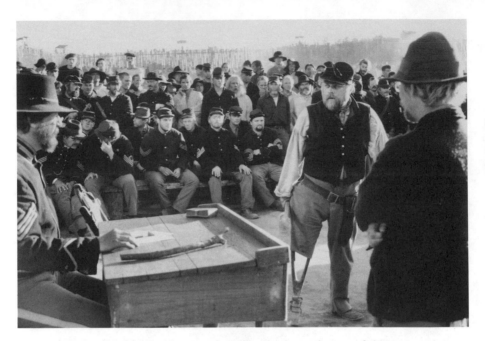

Samson (played by Robert David Hall), who lost a leg in a fight against the Raiders, gives testimony at their trial. The judge (Dale Fetzer) looks on.

JOSIAH (cont.)
May I ask Sergeant Hopkins a question—?

The Foreman waves his permission. Josiah turns to Hopkins—

JOSIAH
Did I understand you to say, sir, that no law applies here . . . ?

HOPKINS
(bounding up)
You did indeed, Corporal. That is the very point!
(to the Jury)
I thank my young friend for his understanding. There is no law here. There are things here—there is starvation here, there is thirst here, there is roasting heat, there is freezing cold, there is disease, there are acts of barbarism and cruelty on all sides—
- (MORE) -

HOPKINS (cont.)
—but law? What law? Whose law?
(a sweeping gesture toward the Towers—)
Rebel law? We do not obey Rebel law! The fact is,
there *is no law here* for my clients—
(the Raiders here)
—to have broken. Therefore they cannot be guilty.
(to Josiah)
I thank you, sir. You are wise beyond your years.

There is general consternation as Hopkins sits triumphantly.

Josiah is the focus of everyone's attention, and even fear. Even Trimble,
even McSpadden and Blackburn and Billy, have to wonder. Then—

JOSIAH
But that cannot be, sir. We live by laws in here—

HOPKINS
The law of *survival*, Corporal!

JOSIAH
We do not stop belonging to the Federal Army just
because we are here—we have our Sergeants—we do
what they command—we maintain order, and disci-
pline—

HOPKINS
(another sweeping gesture)
In here??

JOSIAH
—as best we can: we stand in line to get what little
food they give us—we do not steal from each other—
we do not betray each other to the Rebels—we live
by rules—

Hopkins cuts him off. Turning to the jury—

HOPKINS

I am saying men can be excused if they do extreme
things—necessary things—in order to stay alive in a
place like this—

JOSIAH

The things they did—they knew to be wrong—everyone knows to be wrong—they're against every man's
law and understanding—none of the rest of us did
these things—!

HOPKINS

They did them to live, Corporal! To live!

JOSIAH

All men want to live! But there are some things men
will not do!—won't do!—just to live . . . !

FOREMAN
(stands, angrily!)
What things! That is what we must hear. What was
done here!

TRIMBLE
(now he jumps up)
Murder was done here.

FOREMAN
Then we'll hear about that!

McSpadden and Blackburn look relieved. Josiah has recovered the
ground they thought he'd lost and more.

Trimble, also relieved, nods to the Foreman. He comes back to
Josiah—

TRIMBLE
Tell them (the jury) about Dick Potter, Corporal—

JOSIAH
(this isn't easy. . .)
Dick Potter . . . Dick Potter and his father were the
best fishermen in New Bedford, Massachusetts . . .
He joined up the first summer of the war because he
wanted to . . . because he thought he ought to . . . he
was a good soldier . . . he was shot in both legs at
Antietam and brought here. . . .

DURING THIS, CAMERA STARTS TO DRIFT OFF, past the now-
silent jury, the now-silent and understanding watching Old Prisoners
. . . past McSpadden and Martin Blackburn and the other members of
Our Group . . . and as Josiah's Voice becomes fainter and disappears,
WE SEE THE ENDLESS SILENT FACES, WAITING.

Dissolve To:

Lt. Barrett in the Turkey Roost — Twilight

Looking down, waiting for—

The Jury — Twilight

Favoring the Foreman in a tight circle of the jurors, conferring quietly
with the others. They all agree. He stands in the near dark.

FOREMAN
We've heard enough. Those—

He tosses his head at the non-Ringleaders. . . .

Intercutting as Necessary

The non-Ringleaders wait his judgment.

FOREMAN

—are guilty of theft and low cowardly assault on their
fellows. Give 'em the ball-and-chain or make 'em run
the gauntlet. Every man here who wants gets a swing
at 'em, with your fists—sticks—anything you can get
your hands on—

The Old Prisoners, led by Limber Jim and Samson, ROAR their satis-
faction at the verdict.

Georgie and his fellows are, on balance, relieved. It could have been a
lot worse.

Josiah, now back with McSpadden and Martin Blackburn and Billy,
does not share their delight.

Back to the Foreman . . .

. . . looking at The Six.

FOREMAN

Those six . . .
                    (dismissively)
Hang 'em.

Shots as Necessary

Samson and Limber Jim again roar in delight. . . .

The Six . . .

Munn trembling . . .

Collins defiant, almost unconcerned . . .

COLLINS

Hah!

Josiah and Our Group not participating in the celebration as . . .

CAMERA STARTS BACK INTO HIGH FULL SHOT. The previous ROAR is dwarfed compared to the CHEER THE MEN NOW MAKE. IT REVERBERATES . . . AND THEN FINALLY BEGINS TO DECAY INTO SILENCE AS WE . . .

Dissolve To:

Ext.   Inside the Stockade — Dawn

First light, with the sun just coming over the Stockade wall.

DEAD SILENCE, and then the SOUND OF HAMMERING and CAMERA TILTS DOWN TO SHOW . . .

. . . A group of men building a scaffold (SEE the O'Dea drawing). None of Our Group is among them, but Limber Jim and Samson are, with a vengeance. It's almost done.

The rest of the Prisoners are wide awake, rubbing their naked chests and arms against the morning cold. Many are watching the scaffold-building. Josiah, McSpadden, Martin Blackburn are—and taking no joy from it.

A large group is waiting at the Main Gate. Of Our Group, NOTE ONLY Tyce and Wisnovsky—

—and then the SOUND of the Main Gate opening and Wirz rides in (as a Prisoner described it) "dressed in a suit of white duck, and mounted on his white horse, a conjunction which gained him the appellation of 'Death on a Pale Horse.' Behind him walked the faithful old priest reading the service for the condemned. The six doomed men follow, walking between the double ranks of rebel guards. All came inside the hollow square and halted. . . ."

Limber Jim and Samson on the gallows they helped to build, where the Raiders will soon be hanged.

WIRZ
Prisoners, I return these men to you as good as I got them. You have tried them yourselves and found them guilty. I have had nothing to do with it. I wash my hands of everything connected with them. Do with them as you like and may God have mercy on you and on them.

Squad, about face! Forward, march!

And they leave the Stockade.

The Six look around. They see the faces of their 30,000 Executioners . . .

. . . and then the scaffold.

Two direct quotes:

Some of the estimated two hundred black prisoners at Andersonville, assembled here at the hanging of the Raiders. They included men from the 54th Massachusetts and the 8th and 35th United States Colored Troops. Most were captured at the Battle of Olustee in Florida.

CURTIS
(. . . 'gasped')

My God, men, you don't mean to really hang us up there?

TYCE
(. . . 'laconically')
That seems to be about the size of it.

First Munn, then Curtis and one of the others bolt, running in panic for the Gate.

The other Prisoners, including Tyce, swarm after them, catch them, drag them back fighting and kicking and screaming every inch of the way.

[173]

CLOSE ON COLLINS, captive but unmoving, looking at his weak-kneed friends and their pursuers with disdain. He stands tall, bold and unflinching.

The Old Prisoners march The Six off to the scaffold, Munn and another one or two of The Six pleading, babbling for mercy as they go. 'Just trying to live' . . . 'We're from New York, f'God's sake' . . . 'Can't do this'. . . .

MOVING WITH COLLINS as, with full bravura, he ROARS to his friends . . .

> COLLINS
> This is nothing to worry about! . . . Keep your peckers
> up, boys! We'll have no weakness here . . . ! Did you
> think you were gonna live forever!

Some of the Old Prisoners are enraged at his bravado and YELL at him. MOVING PAST THEM . . .

> OLD PRISONERS
> Get 'em up there . . . Shut him up. . . .
> *(and then a Chant begins and*
> *goes on and on and on . . .)*
> Hang 'em! . . . Hang 'em! . . . Hang 'em! . . . .

The Six pass Josiah, McSpadden, Martin Blackburn, Benton and Tobias, who don't participate in The Chant. This is nothing they want to be a part of. Only Tyce, herding the Six, seems angry and in a vengeful mood.

Mad Matthew runs out to mock the condemned men and dance around them but Josiah catches him gently by the arm—

> JOSIAH
> You don't want to do that, Matthew.

Oh? I don't? And Mad Matthew stops and steps back instantly, docilely.

Munn, one of the Raiders, in manacles as he is led to his hanging.

Many others are not so nice. They call—'Say your prayers, boys—if you know any.' . . . 'Time's almost up.' . . . 'Not so brave this morning, hey, boys?'. . . .

The men are marched through the camp, through all the Prisoners, to and up the scaffold, all the time under a tight hold.

[175]

Left to right, Mad Matthew (Denis Forest) and Josiah Day at the hanging of the Raiders.

Hang 'em! . . . Hang 'em! . . . Hang 'em!

Wisnovsky is one of the Chanters.

So, separately, is 2nd Wisconsin.

MOVING WITH COLLINS, so calm and casual he could be on his way to a picnic. Still ROARING . . .

> COLLINS
> This is Nothing, boys. Doesn't matter a damn, doesn't matter at all. . . .

Hang 'em! . . . Hang 'em! . . . Hang 'em! . . . .

Limber Jim and Samson help with the ropes and blindfolds (meal sacks, in fact) and are not unhappy for the chance.

Samson fixes the rope around Curtis' neck, moves on to Munn.

A couple of The Six pray, led by the Priest. A couple, especially Munn, wriggle and fight and plead. . . .

Not Collins. As they get the sack over his head, he is even grinning at his Hangman, Limber Jim—

> COLLINS
> Let's get this done right, now, Limber Jim. . . .

> LIMBER JIM
> Don't you worry about that—

—as Limber Jim fixes the sack and then tightens the rope, hard.

Now, in a moment of suspended animation, the CHANT STOPS and everything is suddenly quiet. The only sound is the Priest reading the service, but when he finishes and steps back . . .

. . . WE SEE, PANNING MANY FACES, that no one watching is in a charitable mood . . .

. . . except, a hundred yards away, Josiah . . . who alone looks down.

Limber Jim and Samson get at each end of the board on which the Six stand. They look at each other—and nod—

—and yank the board away. The Six fall. Their ropes snap taut.

Long Shot from Outside the Stockade — Day

Not just a LONG SHOT, but the LONGEST POSSIBLE SHOT, SO LONG that The Six and their Priest and Hangmen look like matchsticks against the morning sky. HOLD THE SILENCE.

The hanging of the Raiders.

Fade Out.

Fade In:

Ext.   Inside Andersonville Stockade — Rainy Day

A steady rain. A low mist hangs over the camp. A dreary, monotonous day.

At the Main Gate Seen from the Massachusetts Shebang

New Union Prisoners are being marched in. No Captain Wirz this time. Nobody bothers with ceremony any more.

The Massachusetts Shebang

The Shebang is tattered, in shreds, useless against the rain.

Our Group has deteriorated further. They are dirty, emaciated, grub-infested, shivering.

Two of Our Group—2nd Wisconsin and Tyce—their hair matted, their clothes in rags, looking without great interest at the Main Gate. . . .

> 2ND WISCONSIN
> Fresh fish. Lots of 'em. Means Uncle Billy's Army's close—could be rescued soon.

> TYCE
> Nah—Rebs have to keep ferryin' new boys in, just to keep the population up—so many of us are dying off in here.

Med. Close on Josiah, Martin Blackburn

A few feet away, Josiah is trying to help Martin drink. Martin is shivering and trembling violently as Josiah holds the battered cup to his lips.

> JOSIAH
> It's rainwater, Martin. Good for you. Try . . .

Martin can't keep it down. Instead, coughing, he pulls a loose tooth out of his mouth, looks at it, throws it away—

BLACKBURN

Scurvy—

(then—)

Gums all rotten. Can't even chew the mush anymore—

(and—)

I miss Thomas—don't you?

JOSIAH

(yes)

Sergeant and I were talking about him this morning.

BLACKBURN

Did you know him before the Army?

JOSIAH

We didn't live but ten miles apart but (no)—Sergeant was saying, for a man so strong—we never saw him use his strength in anger. . . .

BLACKBURN

(smiles)

Except to get my banjo back.

JOSIAH

He lived on a farm with all his brothers and sisters. He had a big family.

BLACKBURN

I have six children.

(really?)

Had eight. Two died.

Josiah tries to give Martin another sip of water, but he can't keep it down, while . . .

Tobias and Benton

. . . ten feet away, Tobias and Benton—also filthy and disheveled— share their fantasies as McSpadden, in the background, tries to ig- nore them. . . .

BENTON

She'll start us out with some nice plump chickens
from our own stock—breed 'em ourselves—Rhode
Island Reds—tenderest meat you ever ate—she fries
'em—we'll have 'em with mashed potatoes and
gravy—

TOBIAS

I like my mash potatoes with butter—we make butter
in our spring house—you never had butter like we
churn—

BENTON

You bring the butter. We'll put it on the biscuits—my
mother makes the best biscuits in the world—you just
open 'em up, lift the top off real easy—

TOBIAS

You got honey?

BENTON

'Course we got honey.

TOBIAS

What'll we have after?

BENTON

Pie.

TOBIAS

Apple pie?

BENTON

Apple or cherry.

TOBIAS

Apple *and* cherry.

McSpadden, nearby, has heard as much of this as he can stand . . .

McSPADDEN

Oh, for God Almighty's sake, you want to drive us all
to the lunatic asylum with that kind of talk? Put a
plug in it, for the love of . . .
(calling)
Hey! Friend!

Some of the New Prisoners

Nine or ten of the men who just came in the gate, looking for a place
to set up. Some are from the 17th MAINE, others from the 10th KEN-
TUCKY. NOTE THE CONTRASTS between the new men and Our
Group.

McSPADDEN

Give us the news. Who were you with?

10TH KENTUCKY CORPORAL

We (three or four) was with Uncle Billy Sherman.

17TH MAINE CORPORAL

(We four or five were with) Grant in Virginia.

17TH MAINE PRIVATE

All over Virginia.

McSPADDEN

Makin' it warm for 'em, were you?

10TH KENTUCKY PRIVATE

Warm? Warm?? Let Atlanta burn to the ground! That
warm enough for you?
(amid the laughter)
Now we're heading to Savannah and we'll give them
some of the same, you bet.

Our Group hadn't known that and they react happily. But some of the
new Maine and Kentucky men aren't interested in their own war sto-
ries. Looking around at the ragged men and dismal scene . . .

17TH MAINE PRIVATE
This is Andersonville, huh? Bad as they say?

2ND WISCONSIN
Nope. Worse . . . You boys want to stay with us?

10TH KENTUCKY CORPORAL
(to his friends)
All right with you?
(then—)
Don't see why not.

BENTON
You hear anything about an Exchange?

17TH MAINE CORPORAL
Won't be any Exchange, and that's a fact.

As definite as can be. Our Group looks at each other. Even Josiah . . .

. . . who is still trying to comfort Martin Blackburn on the ground twenty feet away stops and looks up.

It makes some of Our Group unhappy, even belligerent. . . .

TYCE
Well, you seem awful sure of yourself—

17TH MAINE CORPORAL
I should. I was at Sherman's Headquarters the day Grant issued the policy.

Policy? What policy? Our Group doesn't know anything about this. And the 17th Maine Corporal doesn't like having his word questioned. McSpadden smoothes it over . . .

MCSPADDEN
We've been out of touch a while, friend. What policy is that?

[183]

17TH MAINE CORPORAL

Any Reb soldiers he lets go, they just bust their pa-
roles and are back in the line fighting us the next
week—and he's not gonna do it. Says his only job's to
win the war.

17TH MAINE PRIVATE

Rebs are saying as part of an Exchange they wouldn't
send back our colored soldiers. Grant says they're
part of us and without them, it's no deal.

TYCE
(in a fury)
Colored soldiers? We're supposed to die in here for
some damn colored soldiers?!

And some agree with Tyce. But, quietly—

JOSIAH
I say good for Ulysses S. Grant.

And some of the others nod. Damn right. Not Tyce, who is disgusted.

TYCE
Grant know what it's like in here . . . ? !

17TH MAINE CORPORAL
He does for a fact. Someone who got out told him.

Really? Almost afraid to believe, our boys ask—who? Who got out?
Who would that be?

McSpadden looks sharply at Wisnovsky, who is paying the closest possible attention, anxious to hear more.

17TH MAINE CORPORAL
Don't remember the name exactly.
(to the other Maine men)
Any of you boys 'member . . . ?

No—they don't, either.

TOBIAS

What'd he look like?

17TH MAINE CORPORAL

Well, he was sorta tall . . . thin . . . hair has some yel-
low in it . . . older'n me . . . he was a mess . . . all dog-
bit and . . .

And as he gives a good description of Gleason, Our Group is getting
tremendously excited.

BENTON

Could his name have been Gleason?

17TH MAINE CORPORAL

That's it. Gleason, John Gleason. Coal miner fella,
from Pennsylvania . . . He told Uncle Billy. . . .

Sherman! John got to Uncle Billy Sherman! . . . Our men, particularly
the Pennsylvania men, are laughing and dancing and crying and hugging each other . . .

. . . and McSpadden comes to Wisnovsky and puts a hand on his shoulder. Wisnovsky, full of wonder, can only nod, very moved.

But twenty feet away, Martin Blackburn isn't celebrating. He is in Josiah's arms and, with the last of his strength, and privately, only for Josiah, and without complaint or self-pity . . .

BLACKBURN

Means we're going to die in here, Josie.

JOSIAH

Just because no Exchange—you heard how the Army's doing—first Atlanta, then Savannah—maybe
we'll be rescued—

BLACKBURN

You remember the map . . .
                    (yes . . .)
Savannah's toward the sea. We're inland. Army's go-
ing the other way.
                    (then—)
Would you send a letter to my wife and children? . . .
        (as Josiah goes for his pencil and paper)
And make sure I have a toe tag? . . . You go out to the
Dead House without a toe tag, how's anyone sup-
posed to know where you're buried—?

As Josiah nods, Tobias and Benton break away from the celebration to
come give Martin and Josiah the good news . . .

TOBIAS

Didja hear, Martin!

BENTON

John made it! He got to Sherman! He said he would
and he . . . !

BLACKBURN

Get my banjo. I'll play dancin' music for you.

He smiles weakly at them. They run off to the Shebang for the banjo
while the celebration goes on around them. Only Martin and Josiah
know a different truth. STARTING OVER JOSIAH AND MARTIN,
with a BANJO COMING IN WITH SLOW, MOVING DANCE MU-
SIC OVER . . .

JOSIAH'S VOICE OVER

We know now we are coming to the end of our time
here, one way or the other. . . .

. . . as the happy boys, Tobias and Benton, come running back INTO
SHOT with Martin's banjo but slow uncertainly when they see he is
asleep or unconscious, or dead, and in no condition to play it . . .

As the Camera Starts a Slow Pan Away . . .

. . . past a few happy celebrants, who are winding down . . .

. . . to the always, and increasingly, dismal, dreary camp, as the rain slows and stops, leaving the near-naked men miserable and shaking in the cold . . .

. . . as Josiah's VOICE continues with its growing understanding . . .

> JOSIAH'S VOICE OVER
> Wars end . . . and there are signs all around us that this war too will someday end, and soon, with the Rebellion crushed and our great Cause victorious . . . 'though until that day it still will go very hard on the men. . . .

A couple of Prisoners are nibbling tiny pieces of dough, but most have nothing, nor seemingly much interest in food. . . .

> JOSIAH'S VOICE OVER
> The rations have been cut, and cut again, to scarcely four ounces of rough unbolted cornmeal, including cob and husk, each day. The cob tears a man's bowels all to pieces and some choose to die rather than eat it . . .

> . . . which may be more meanness on the Rebels' part or—'though none of the boys thinks so—may be that there is not enough food for the Rebels to feed themselves and feed us, too . . .

During the Above

THE PANNING CAMERA has brought us past the guard towers with their young and old Sentinels . . .

. . . and scarcely a day goes by when one of us isn't shot for fear or sport or malice when we cross or approach too near the Deadline. . . .

But mostly they seem not to know we are here or even care.

. . . and now past Limber Jim who has boosted young Patrick onto his shoulders, where he is standing, flailing at low-flying birds, trying to knock one out of the sky with a stick as Limber Jim staggers around and fights for balance. . . .

The Main Gate

. . . and past them to the Main Gate, which now opens. A flatbed cart is wheeled in by slaves under the direction of Lt. Barrett . . .

. . . and Wirz and the CONFEDERATE COLONEL O'NEIL come inside the gate and wait for it to be put in position. When it is, both Wirz and O'Neil climb onto the cart and Wirz nods to Lt. Barrett, who calls loudly—

LT. BARRETT

You Yankees—you listen now! Colonel's got somethin' real important to tell you all—

—so Sergeants, you get your men down here double quick now.

At the Massachusetts Shebang

Josiah, who has been writing, finishes a sentence before looking over to McSpadden.

JOSIAH
Want me to go down there for you, Sergeant?

MCSPADDEN
Nah—I'm starting to feel my old First Sergeant's self again—we'll go together—I can listen to their nonsense well as you can.

Josiah helps him up and they take a few steps toward the cart but stop when they see—

—2nd Wisconsin lying curled up, near-lifeless in the mud. Tobias is sitting with him.

MCSPADDEN
You all right, Wisconsin?

TOBIAS
Lost his last three days' rations in that keno game the 33rd New Jersey runs—

MCSPADDEN
Those robbers—

2ND WISCONSIN
My own fault—

JOSIAH
We don't have anything—won't 'til the food cart comes tomorrow—

2ND WISCONSIN
Own fault—

MCSPADDEN
C'mon—walk with us—can you?

2nd Wisconsin struggles up and joins the others, including even Martin Blackburn, as they start down to the Main Gate. The men are grousing, limping, without great interest and not expecting much as they follow McSpadden and Josiah.

Full Shot

From all parts of the Stockade, the Prisoners come down to the Main Gate—

—and assemble in ragged Detachments, each of about 270 men, behind their Sergeants and in front of the flatbed cart—

—where Wirz and O'Neil wait.

Closer Shot of Our Group

Lined up raggedly, inattentively, behind Sergeant McSpadden.

Josiah has to hold Martin upright. Tobias holds 2nd Wisconsin.

Med. Shot on Wirz, O'Neil

When they see that all the Prisoners are in place . . .

> WIRZ
> The Colonel comes with an important message for all of you.
>
> Colonel O'Neil. . . .

> O'NEIL
> You men—you Prisoners—I want to speak to you about your situation. It must be clear to you now that your Government has cruelly abandoned you. As you know—
>
> —they have turned down all our efforts to exchange you. They know of your suffering—
> - (MORE) -

O'NEIL (cont.)
—which, 'though terrible, is no worse than our men
are suffering in Northern Prisons—

Reaction Shots in the Ranks

Not knowing where O'Neil is going, not caring, not believing a word
he's saying. Even Limber Jim, even little Patrick next to him, are not
paying attention as . . .

Their POV of O'Neil

O'NEIL
—and they know, as we all do, that you have already
endured far more than should be expected of you.

And now that your Government has no more use for
you, you are being thrown aside to starve and die.
That being so—

—and with the Southern Confederacy certain to suc-
ceed and gain its independence in only a few more
months . . .

Some of the men in the ranks, like Tyce, roll their eyes. Most don't
waste the energy.

O'NEIL
. . . I make you all this offer. If you join our army, and
if you serve it faithfully to the end, you will receive
the same rewards as the rest of our soldiers. You will
be taken out of here at once—

—today, this minute—

—clothed and fed, given a good cash bounty and, at
the conclusion of the war, receive a land warrant for
a nice farm.

DURING THE ABOVE, a transformation starts to overtake the men in the ranks. They start to listen and to look at each other. It is hard to know what they are thinking, but they are paying attention.

The Colonel continues . . .

> O'NEIL
>
> That is our offer.
>
> What is your answer?

At first, nothing. The men just look at each other. Then—

Med. Shot on Sergeant McSpadden

Facing the speaker, with his Detachment at his back. He takes two steps forward.

> McSPADDEN
>
> Colonel, sir!
>
> Sergeant James Dudley McSpadden, 19th Massachu-setts Volunteers, Sir!
>
> I have the honor to speak for my Detachment, Sir!
>
> Attention, First Detachment! About—
>
> Face!

Full Shot on McSpadden's Detachment

In a brilliant, precise, military maneuver, the men turn as one on their heels. Josiah does it perfectly. Martin Blackburn stumbles badly but makes it with Josiah's help. Tobias helps 2nd Wisconsin.

And—they are a rabble no longer.

MCSPADDEN
Forward—march!

They march off, back into camp, their heads held high. As they pass in front of the next column, where Samson stands—

SAMSON
Three cheers for Sergeant McSpadden!

All the men in all the Detachments—everyone of them—give a . . .

ALL THE MEN
Hip hip, hooray!

Another Sergeant (Slater)

And his men, including Limber Jim and Patrick, watching with pride and joining in the cheer for McSpadden. When McSpadden's men are past, he faces the Confederate officers on the cart and calls—

SERGEANT SLATER
Attention, Second Detachment! About—

Face!

And as they proudly, crisply, turn—

SERGEANT SLATER
Forward—march!

His Detachment marches away from—

—the infuriated O'Neil and Wirz—

—as all the other Sergeants and all the other Detachments do the same in order until no one is left facing the speaker, and all he can see is—

—their thousand backs marching away from him in military cadence, as the MUSIC comes in OVER . . .

—and he cannot see the proud, smiling faces of Josiah and Billy and Martin Blackburn, of Tobias and 2nd Wisconsin and Benton, of Limber Jim and Samson and little Patrick Shay, of Tyce and the others—

—and most of all McSpadden, in CLOSE SHOT, limping and battered but now very much again a Sergeant . . .

. . . and the CAMERA HOLDS McSPADDEN AND THE MARCHING MEN AND WE SLOWLY START TO LOSE THEM INTO . . .

THE SOUND of a rising wind OVER the White Screen.

White Out.

White In:

Ext.   Near the Massachusetts Shebang — Day

A corpse, frozen in a sitting position—what was called at the time "the attitude(s) of death"—his dead eyes open. The WIND CONTINUES OVER . . .

A couple of near-naked Prisoners fight each other weakly for his shirt and pants. They have no strength to fight with, but still . . .

Josiah Foreground of the Fighting Men

Josiah is twenty feet away, in rags and tatters and with more hair and wild beard. He briefly looks at the men fighting over the corpse, and then turns back to writing with his pencil stub, concentrating on trying to get his stiff fingers to work.

[194]

JOSIAH'S VOICE OVER

Now that it is so cold, we fight each morning to steal
rags from the newly-dead, to cover ourselves, and
fight also for the right to carry them out to the Dead
House, where it's possible sometimes to find a scrap
of wood to make a fire that will keep us another day
or two—

Martin Blackburn is lying at his side, barely breathing, looking up at
the grey sky. Tobias and Benton are nearby.

Josiah looks off to where a dozen scrawny men are running madly
around in a tight knot, chasing something—all now going here, all
now there, veering off again until finally they stop and stomp the
ground and cheer and one triumphantly holds up a what? A tiny ball
of grey something at the end of a grey string. . . .

Looking back from the knot of triumphant men to his writing as—

JOSIAH'S VOICE OVER

—though all there is now to eat are the rats we sometimes catch, and the boys are so starved they most
times don't wait to cook 'em anyway.

We heard yesterday a few of the men sneaked out to
accept the Rebels' offer to join their army. Poor dismal wretches, to have fallen so far. . . .

Josiah looks over to see that Martin is slipping away. He puts his pencil
down and gently rubs Martin's bare feet and breathes on them.

Martin can only blink his thanks.

Josiah picks up his pencil and starts writing again as the WIND
BLOWS OVER his weakened VOICE. . . .

JOSIAH'S VOICE OVER

I have tried to keep my hopes up all these months but,
now I know there is no hope, I pray whoever finds
- (MORE) -

these letters will take them to you as a keepsake of
your son Josiah Day. You will know I do not mind
dying, for I know the Union must be saved and one
man's life is no great price to pay for so great a Cause
as that.

But if whoever finds these letters needs burn them to
keep warm, I have no quarrel with him.

He looks up to SEE—

The Main Gate From Josiah's POV

It's opening.

Back to Josiah

He puts his letter down and says to Martin—

> JOSIAH
> Food cart's here, Martin. I'll bring you something.

Again, Martin blinks without moving and—

—Josiah stumbles a few yards down toward the food cart.

Coming up toward him, in a fury, is his old friend Limber Jim, also
looking gaunter and far worse than before.

> LIMBER JIM
> Some more of the "boys"—some more of the "boys"
> sneaked out last night—took the Rebs' offer—joined
> up with them—walked right out the gate—

Josiah hears. He wishes it weren't so and yet . . . he doesn't have it in
him to be so angry. Instead he puts a consoling hand on Limber Jim's

shoulder. And maybe he would say something, but his attention is diverted by . . .

Main Gate From Josiah's POV

—as Wirz comes in at the head of his guard, on foot, and clambers onto the food cart. Prisoners pay attention as—

> WIRZ
> So—gather 'round. I have good news for you. It will make you very happy. You are being exchanged, starting today, every one of you, starting right now, this morning . . . You see? All this time I was right. Go tell the rest—everyone is exchanged—the train leaves in two hours—

> The gate is open, you see?

And this time the men believe him, but most do not have the strength to do anything about it.

One who does is Limber Jim, who shouts to the heavens and runs off to get his things.

Josiah limps back to Martin.

> JOSIAH
> Martin . . . ! Martin . . . ! We're exchanged . . .

But when he gets there, Martin is dead, eyes and toothless mouth open to the sky, the flies already having possession of him . . .

. . . and as Tobias and Benton embrace and dance . . .

. . . and the rest of the Camp starts to come alive with GROWING CHEERS being carried on the wind in the distance . . .

. . . and Limber Jim throws Patrick straight up in the air, and catches him as he comes down . . .

. . . Josiah sits next to Martin, folds Martin's hands across his chest, tries to wave the flies away from him . . .

. . . and then writes *Martin Blackburn, 184 Pa.* on a scrap of paper, takes a loose thread from his own or Martin's shirt, ties the paper around Martin's big toe . . .

. . . and then looks around and does not join the celebration. HOLD Josiah and the SOUND of the WIND and then INTERCUT—

Josiah's POV

—looking at his friends, at his home, trying to fix it all in his heart and mind, trying to understand it.

We see McSpadden limp out of the Shebang, and some of the others both near and far, Billy, Tyce, Limber Jim and Patrick, Samson, Old Prisoners blinking in the sun.

Josiah looks up at them stumbling and dancing around and tries to remember all that has happened and feels apart, living not in freedom but in memory.

Finally he gets up to stand with McSpadden and they watch as everyone heads for the Main Gate. But he does not move at first, even when McSpadden suggests it. A last look around . . .

. . . and then he takes Martin Blackburn's feet and tells McSpadden to take the arms . . .

. . . and Josiah and McSpadden start down to the Main Gate carrying their burden between them. Others, quicker and happier, pass them.

At the Main Gate

Wirz and Lt. Barrett and a few armed guards stand at the gate, almost a Reviewing Line, watching the men go out past them. They look at the men. Some but by no means most of the men look back—in anger, like Tyce and Billy and Limber Jim, or triumphantly, like Tobias and Benton, or even cheerfully, like little Patrick and Mad Matthew.

Resume Josiah, McSpadden

Approaching the Main Gate, carrying Martin Blackburn, as others pass them. . . .

> JOSIAH'S VOICE OVER
> It turned out not to be true. We weren't yet free. It was only that the Rebels had heard Sherman's Army was coming to save us, and this was a trick, a ruse to get us to walk to their train—

As they pass the Confederate Officers and go out the gate—

> JOSIAH'S VOICE OVER
> —where we were taken, under guard, to other prison camps until the war ended.

> But the one we were taken to was not so bad as Andersonville, and we all of us survived it, excepting only two of the Indiana boys and one from Kentucky—

CAMERA PULLS UP INTO A HIGH SHOT as, once outside the gate, Josiah and McSpadden, alone and unaccompanied, diverge from the others to carry Martin Blackburn to the Dead House—

—where they gently lay him down. McSpadden folds Martin's hands across his chest. Josiah makes sure his toe tag is secure. They stay with him a long silent moment. Then—

—as all the other Prisoners continue out the Main Gate, heading in the direction of the train, down the road they'd first come on, McSpadden, and a moment later Josiah, get up to join them. As they walk away from the Dead House and from the Stockade, CAMERA PULLS UP TO SHOW them joining the others, becoming a part of the infinitely long line. FOLLOW THEM and then TIME DISSOLVE TO . . .

Ext. Inside the Stockade — Day

The whole prison, now deserted. Not a living soul here—

—only the battered shebangs, the empty towers, the waste and loss and emptiness and hollowness everywhere visible.

A low thin ground fog gives us the vision of Hell.

CAMERA PANS SLOWLY AS, OVER THIS, WE HEAR ONLY THE WIND . . .

. . . UNTIL WE HEAR THE SOUND OF MARTIN BLACKBURN'S BANJO FADE SOFTLY IN . . .

. . . AS THE CAMERA STARTS A SLOW PULLBACK . . .

. . . AND WE GO HIGHER AND FURTHER AWAY until WE SEE THE WHOLE STOCKADE empty and grey below us.

The BANJO continues softly into a . . .

Dissolve To:

Ext. Andersonville Cemetery — Today

The hallowed ground, now a green field, finally at peace.

Close by the field, among beautiful trees and flowers, the gravestones and monuments go on, seemingly forever.

We see, FIRST AND CLOSELY, Martin Blackburn's stone and then WIDEN and MOVE AMONG the other graves, the thousands of them.

THREE CARDS FADE ON AND OFF, SUPERIMPOSED OVER THE GRAVESTONES. . . .

In 1864–5, more than 45,000 Union Soldiers were imprisoned in Andersonville.

12,914 died and are buried there.

Captain Wirz was put on trial after the war and was hanged, the only person to be executed after the Civil War for War Crimes.

The BANJO plays on over the endless, timeless gravestones.

Fade Out.

The End

ABOUT THE AUTHOR

David W. Rintels is the author of the Broadway stage play *Clarence Darrow* starring Henry Fonda, and such award-winning television programs as *Sakharov* starring Jason Robards and Glenda Jackson, *Fear on Trial* with George C. Scott, and *The Last Best Year* with Mary Tyler Moore and Bernadette Peters. He is the writer-producer of *World War II: When Lions Roared* starring Michael Caine, Bob Hoskins and John Lithgow, *Day One* with Brian Dennehy, David Strathairn and Hume Cronyn, and *Gideon's Trumpet* starring Henry Fonda and John Houseman, and he has produced such programs as *My Antonia*, *The Execution of Raymond Graham* and *The Oldest Living Graduate*. He has won three Emmy Awards, has been named Television Producer of the Year by the Producers Guild of America, and has three times won Outstanding Script of the Year honors from the Writers Guild of America.

Mr. Rintels and his wife Victoria Riskin, a writer and producer, live in West Los Angeles, California.